CW00493425

THE PASTA MAN

FOR MIKOLAJ, WHO STARTED
ME ON THIS ADVENTURE

THE PASTA MAN

THE ART OF MAKING SPECTACULAR PASTA, WITH 40 RECIPES

mateo zielonka

Photography by India Hobson

Hardie Grant

QUADRILLE

CONTENTS

INTRODUCTION

For my sixteenth birthday my brother Jakub bought me a copy of *The Sopranos Family Cookbook*. I was obsessed with watching the TV series and I particularly loved the big, noisy family dinners, with enormous bowls of food to be shared among all the people crowded around the table. I remember the generous servings of pasta, the bottles of wine, the meals that seemed to go on forever. I wanted to eat at Artie Bucco's restaurant Vesuvio, or at the sandwich shop with the red-and-white-checked tablecloths. I never cooked anything from that book – for a start, some of the ingredients were either unobtainable or just too expensive – but it introduced me to a food culture that I've come to love.

Who knows where that book is now? Nearly ten years later, when I arrived in London for a holiday, I just had my backpack with enough clothes for a couple of weeks. I had no idea that I wouldn't return home to Poland. Instead, I found a job washing dishes in a restaurant kitchen. I'd come to visit my friend Mikolaj who worked at Mishkins, a New York-style Jewish deli in Covent Garden, and I ended up working there too.

It was a slightly reckless decision as I had a much better job at home in Poland and I didn't even speak English. But there was something about the kitchen that I just loved. Maybe it was a throwback to Artie Bucco's place. The cosmopolitan team, the camaraderie, the crazy demands and the adrenaline, not to mention the introduction to a completely different kind of food. I felt at home there and I wanted to stay, but I didn't want to wash up forever.

I started to help out with other kitchen tasks. Tim, the head chef, took me under his wing and I learned about food prep and, probably even more crucially, how to speak better English. Nearly all the words I learned initially were related to ingredients and kitchen utensils, or instructions like, 'Run to Tesco's!' – an almost daily cry when we ran out of something crucial.

Tim introduced me to Florence Knight, who was just about to open Polpetto, another restaurant in the same group. I went to be a commis chef in her kitchen, and it was there that I learned all about the beautiful produce and authentic flavours of the best Italian cooking. I loved that job so much that I tried to be first in the kitchen every day as well as last out at night. It was amazing, walking through the narrow streets of Soho at either end of the day; there was always something crazy happening.

My next job was at Padella, which started as a cool concept place offering small plates of hand-made pasta, and is now one of the best-known pasta restaurants in London. It was there that I met the two most important people in my pasta career: head chef Ray O'Connor and sous chef Tom Wakefield. They taught me how to make pasta, how to roll and shape it, how to cook it to perfection, and that is where I truly fell in love with it.

I bought myself a small pasta machine so that I could make fresh dough at home. We ate an awful lot of pasta because I became obsessed with making it (they do say 'never trust a skinny chef'). It's such a simple thing to make, just flour and eggs, but there's nothing more satisfying than bringing the dough together, then watching it roll out of the machine in beautiful, neat strands ready to cook for supper.

Once I'd learned the basics, I started to look for new ideas. That is when I met Konrad, a fellow chef from Poland, who makes beautiful, fresh coloured pastas. We talked about colours and shapes, and after that I found inspiration everywhere: social media, sculptures at Tate Modern, patterns in wood, the veg patch…

Now I run the restaurant at 180 The Strand for The Store X, a collaborative studio and arts space in central London, and of course pasta is on the menu every day. Both here and on Instagram, where I'm always posting pictures of my pasta, people have started to call me 'The Pasta Man'. At its best, social media introduces you to people who share your passion, and it's always been an amazing source of friendship and inspiration for me. I like nothing more than reading people's food stories – whether it's remembering sharing pasta with their grandparents, or learning to cook it with their own children – and it always makes me happy when they post pictures of the pasta they've made at home.

Now, I want to share my pasta with you. In this book you will find over 40 recipes, mostly Italian-style, but some that weave in my own favourite flavours and ingredients. I hope everyone will find something new to try, as well as a few old favourites.

Of course, I'm also going to show you how to make multi-coloured pasta – green dough made from spinach, a gorgeous jewel-red beetroot (beet) dough, and a rich egg dough, as well as vegan semolina versions. You will learn to make some of the classic pasta shapes as well as beautiful filled pasta – some easy, some a little tricky, but with practice, it will become as simple as folding a paper fan, I promise. The step-by-step photos will guide you and you can also watch my how-to videos on my website and on Instagram.

I hope you will enjoy making pasta as much as I do. Remember to let me know how you get on!

Matt x

@mateo.zielonka
www.mateopasta.com

EQUIPMENT

Let's start with the essentials. You will need a pasta machine, otherwise you'll be limited in what you can make, but you don't need very much more than that, and some things you'll already have in your kitchen. This list will help you to get started.

PASTA MACHINE
If you haven't got one already, it's really worth the investment, as once you've made your own fresh pasta you'll be hooked. I recommend a Marcato Atlas 180 pasta machine, as it's wider than most and is a good, solid machine. You will need a pasta machine to make all the pastas in this book, with the exception of the vegan *malloreddus* and *capunti*.

RAVIOLI CUTTER
This will help to seal the edges of filled pastas such as *ravioli*, *triangoli* or *agnolotti del plin*, and create the decorative edges characteristic of these shapes. Good *ravioli* cutters have a brass cutting wheel and are something of an investment, but if you want to make pasta regularly they are well worth it.

One thing I have to stress here: do not wash either your pasta machine or *ravioli* cutter. Just let them dry out after use and then clean with a soft brush or a damp cloth. If you wash them, the flour that remains in them will clog up and ruin the machine and the cutter. A chef once put my pasta machine in the dishwasher and – *mamma mia!* – it was a mess.

GARGANELLI OR CAVAROLA BOARD
I use this board to make *garganelli*, *malloreddus* and *capunti*, though I will also explain in these recipes how to make them without the board, using a fork or a Microplane grater instead. You can find boards online – they are quite cheap, unless you choose a specialist maker.

CHITARRA BOX
This is probably only necessary for serious pasta-makers, as it is only used for one type of pasta. It's also quite a large box to store. You can find a *chitarra* box online if you decide to try making this shape.

GENERAL KITCHEN ITEMS

- A food processor will make quick work of pasta dough, as well as being useful for sauces, pesto, breadcrumbs (*pangrattato*) and to whip-up ricotta.

- A rolling pin.

- A good knife.

- A ruler to measure squares and ribbons of pasta.

- A pastry or ring cutter to cut circles for *culurgiones* or patterned pasta dough.

- A piping bag with a narrow opening for filling pasta. This can help to manage softer fillings like ricotta and pumpkin as it is compressed a little through the nozzle (but I just use a teaspoon instead).

- A dough scraper really helps to get the dough off your work surface when you have finished. I also use it to help shape one or two of the pasta doughs.

- A large pan to cook the pasta in – I generally use a stainless-steel 6-litre/12½-US pint pan. I don't use a specialist pasta pan as I don't think they're particularly useful.

- A wide saucepan to cook sauces, approximately 25cm/10in in diameter. Bear in mind that you'll be transferring the cooked pasta to the sauce, so you need enough room to combine the two.

INGREDIENTS

I always have the following items in my store cupboard or fridge – as you never know when there's going to be a pasta emergency. All you really need is pasta, olive oil and Parmesan, and dinner is on the table.

ITALIAN 00 FLOUR
This is really finely milled flour that has been ground twice – it is almost the texture of icing (powdered) sugar – and it gives you a beautifully smooth, pliable dough. This flour is my absolute favourite for making egg dough pasta.

I recommend the flour and semolina made by Molino Pasini near Modena, northern Italy. I'm lucky enough to find it in my local market in Dorset, UK, and you should be able to track it down wherever you are.

FINE & COARSE SEMOLINA
Use fine semolina (sometimes called 'semola'), which is the equivalent of 00 Italian wheat flour, to make vegan pasta dough.

Use coarse semolina for dusting pasta dough, either to dry out the pasta as you work, if needed, or to prevent the pasta sticking together after you've shaped it. I re-use any semolina that's left behind after lifting the pasta from the tray; sifted to remove any pieces of pasta and stored in a container, it can be used three or four times before you discard it.

EGGS
I am often asked why my pasta has such a vibrant colour. That lovely golden tone comes from using free-range rich-yolk eggs from St Ewe's in Cornwall (these are widely available in the UK, but if you can't find them look for eggs that say 'rich yolk' on the box). The St Ewe's hens have been fed with natural, safe pigments, including extract of marigold petals, which produces the golden yolks.

I give two recipes for egg dough in this book. One is a classic pasta dough (page 26); the second uses extra egg yolks (page 27), which produces a richer, golden colour. You will end up with leftover egg whites, so your best bet is to become a wizard at making meringues.

I always use medium eggs in my recipes.

OLIVE OIL

I love good-quality extra-virgin olive oil and use it for both cooking sauces and for finishing the pasta – an extra drizzle of oil can really lift a dish. I'm a big fan of Nicolas Alziari olive oil, which is produced in Provence in the south of France. Their elegant cans of oil look pretty on the kitchen shelf, too.

PARMESAN

Look out for *Parmigiano-Reggiano* – authentic cows' milk cheese from northern Italy aged for a minimum of 12 months. This grainy, complex, sharp cheese is used to finish pasta dishes and occasionally added to pasta sauces. The more mature Parmesan has an even more intense flavour, but I don't use it for cooking and save it for the cheese board.

Save any Parmesan rinds you have and freeze them. You can then use them in a risotto or soup stock (broth) to add a beautiful tangy flavour.

PECORINO ROMANO

This is a hard sheep's-milk cheese, which is now generally produced in Sardinia. I find the flavour softer and slightly creamier than Parmesan and, for me, it's just as good for finishing a dish.

SALT

I use fine sea salt or table salt in pasta cooking water because it has a more intense flavour and it's simply cheaper to use. Why waste beautiful sea salt flakes in cooking water? I always use salt flakes to finish a dish, however.

Note: I only give seasoning quantities in recipes where a particular amount is required, otherwise it's best left to your own personal taste. Always check the seasoning before you serve a finished dish.

DRIED PASTA

Choose a pasta that is made with only two ingredients – water and durum wheat (semolina) – and labelled 'bronze extruded' or '*trafila ruvida di bronzo*'. This means that the pasta is formed through a bronze die, giving it a rough, porous surface, which helps to carry the sauce.

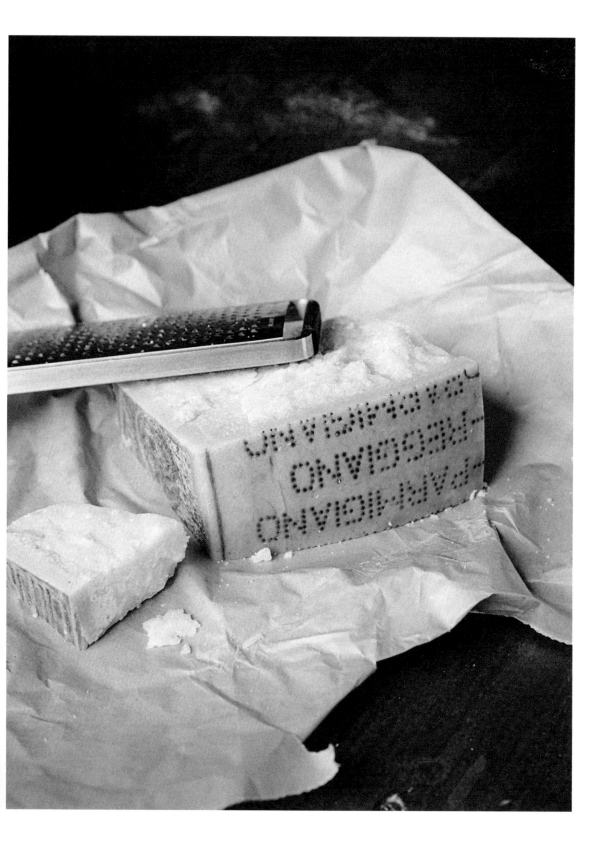

HOW TO COOK PASTA

Everyone knows how to cook pasta, don't they? Well, they think they do, but I've eaten overcooked or sticky pasta even in fancy restaurants, so it's worth going over the general rules to make sure you get it just right.

The most important advice I can give you is to make sure your sauce is cooked and ready when you start boiling your fresh pasta; this avoids you overcooking the pasta while you wait for the sauce. Follow these steps and you'll soon be cooking pasta like an Italian *nonna*!

THE COOKING WATER

You should use a large pan to cook your fresh pasta as the water should be able to circulate around the pasta, otherwise it will not cook evenly and may clump together. I use about 4 litres/8½ US pints of water for four portions of pasta – so, 1 litre/2 US pints for every 100g/3½oz of pasta.

It is really important to season the water heavily. There's no salt in pasta – it's just flour and egg – so the seasoning comes from the cooking water and from the sauce it's served with. I add table salt or fine sea salt to the water once it's boiling (if you add the salt to cold water it simply takes longer to boil – also, I love the whoosh of the boiling water when you add salt to it). I don't recommend a particular quantity of salt as salts actually vary in flavour and intensity, but what I can tell you is that the water should taste as salty as sea water.

COOKING FRESH RIBBON PASTA

Always drop the pasta into the water when it's boiling steadily. If you're impatient and add it too soon, the pasta won't cook perfectly.

I add cooked pasta to the sauce, rather than adding the sauce to the pasta. I use kitchen tongs to lift the long ribbons out of the cooking water and into the sauce – you don't want to drain it too well, as the moist pasta carries some of the lovely starchy cooking water with it and helps the sauce cling to each strand.

Always reserve a generous jugful of cooking water to further loosen the sauce – you need more than you think, as the cooked pasta continues to absorb liquid when combined with the sauce. Add a ladleful at a time.

I like to toss the pasta, which is why I generally cook sauces in a wide, shallow pan, but you can also use tongs or a spatula to simply turn it and make sure it is well coated in the sauce.

As ever, taste the finished dish to check that you like the texture and the seasoning, and adjust it with more salt or cooking water if needed before serving.

COOKING FILLED PASTA

When you've spent an hour or two shaping lovely *ravioli* or *cappelletti*, the last thing you want to do is watch them split open in a crowded saucepan. You may find it easier to cook the pasta in two batches, one after the other, transferring each batch to the sauce once cooked. It's probably best to use one large pan if you can, but work as quickly and carefully as possible, dropping the pasta into the water in small handfuls so that it cooks evenly.

Once the pasta is cooked, lift it out of the water using a slotted spoon, reserving the cooking water until you've combined the pasta with the sauce. The sauce may need loosening, but add the water a little at a time, moving the pasta gently around the pan so that the parcels don't split.

COOKING DRIED PASTA

As with fresh pasta, add dried pasta to steadily boiling salted water. Follow the cooking time specified on the packet, but check it a minute or two before the time stated, to ensure that it retains some bite – it will finish cooking in the accompanying sauce anyway. If you prefer your pasta a little softer than *al dente*, just cook it for a bit longer.

Don't leave the pasta sitting in the cooking water. Drain it straight away by tipping it into a colander or sieve placed over a bowl, so you can catch the cooking water to use for loosening the sauce.

You can usually buy dried *lasagne* sheets that are ready to use and don't need to be blanched. Just make sure there is enough liquid in the sauce to cook the pasta in the oven. If the sauce looks a little dry, add a small amount of cow's milk or oat milk to the white sauce, or a bit of warm water to the tomato sauce.

FREEZING PASTA

You can freeze pasta, but it tends to dry out a bit, so I never leave it in the freezer for longer than two weeks.

To freeze the dough, wrap it tightly in clingfilm (plastic wrap). Take it out of the freezer the evening before you want to use it and leave it to defrost in the fridge. The dough will have a slightly different consistency when you come to roll it, but don't worry; if it crumbles as you put it through the machine, press it together with your hands, then try rolling it again.

I only really recommend freezing filled pastas, never the ribbon pastas; they tend to crumble or break once defrosted and they don't look as appealing as they should. Filled shapes are best frozen on a tray or baking sheet and then, once frozen, transferred to a container and returned to the freezer. You can cook filled pasta from frozen – just drop them straight into boiling salted water and allow an extra minute's cooking time.

HOW TO FINISH YOUR PASTA DISH

Take the trouble to warm your plates or pasta bowls before serving. Pasta can cool quite rapidly, so a warmed dish will always help.

Parmesan is the perfect way to finish pasta, but *pangrattato* (page 153) and nutritional yeast are great alternatives for adding umami flavour. These options are not only for vegans – I often use a combination.

You can also make a simple herb salsa dressed with a little olive oil to finish your pasta (page 151).

A real indulgence is to add half a creamy burrata – a delicate Italian cows' milk cheese made from mozzarella and cream – to a portion of pasta. This is best topped with a little sea salt, fresh black pepper and a drizzle of olive oil.

I'm also very fond of finishing a meal with a piece of bread. In Italy, this is called *fare la scarpetta* – using a piece of soft bread to mop up your plate, especially after a creamy pasta sauce.

Try to balance a meal of pasta with a bowl of greens. I think it's nice to keep it simple, just some blanched broccoli or a fresh green salad. And of course, a glass of wine or beer is never a bad idea!

THE DOUGHS

CLASSIC EGG DOUGH

This is the classic pasta recipe followed by generations of Italian families, using whole eggs and Italian 00 flour, and it is the best place to start learning how to make fresh pasta. You will end up with a soft yellow dough, ready to shape into ribbons or little parcels. If, when you are kneading the dough, it feels quite stiff and difficult to work, don't give up. It will become more elastic the more you work it, the structure will improve, and it will soften further in the fridge as the moisture of the egg loosens the dough.

300g/2⅓ cups Italian 00 flour
3 eggs

**MAKES 400G/14OZ,
ENOUGH TO SERVE 4**

Place the flour on a clean work surface or board and shape it into a mound. Make a well in the centre and crack the eggs into the middle.

Using a fork, break the egg yolks and start to gently whisk them. Draw in the flour a little at a time and continue to combine with the fork (pages 28–9).

When everything starts to come together, use your hands to knead the dough for 8–10 minutes until smooth. Use the heel of one hand to push the dough away from you, and use your other hand to turn it 90 degrees after each knead – you will soon develop a lovely rhythm.

When the dough is smooth, form it into a flat disc (this will be much easier to roll out later). Wrap it tightly in clingfilm (plastic wrap) and rest in the fridge for at least 30 minutes, or ideally overnight. Resting makes the structure of the dough smoother and more pliable, so it's much easier to roll out and shape.

USING A FOOD PROCESSOR
You can also make pasta dough in a food processor – it's really quick and easy, though I actually prefer to make it by hand, especially at home. (I like listening to music and kneading to the rhythm of some 80s classics!)

Place the flour in the processor bowl and secure the lid. Start the machine, then pour the eggs into the funnel.

Mix for 30 seconds, until the dough has the consistency of fine breadcrumbs.

Tip onto a board or into a bowl and use your hands to bring the mixture together to form a neat disc. Wrap the dough tightly in clingfilm (plastic wrap) and refrigerate, as above.

RICH EGG DOUGH

If you want a rich yellow pasta, use more egg yolks. If you're lucky enough to find eggs that have extra-rich yolks, this will help create a vibrant, sunny colour that looks really appealing. My kind of gold. The additional yolks make the dough more pliable when you are kneading it, and slightly drier when you come to roll it out. Don't waste the egg whites – use them to make meringue, pavlova or to add to scrambled eggs.

280g/2¼ cups Italian 00 flour
2 eggs, plus 4 egg yolks

**MAKES 400G/14OZ.
ENOUGH TO SERVE 4**

Follow steps 1–4 of the classic egg dough recipe, opposite, adding the extra yolks with the eggs. You can make this by hand or using a food processor.

GLUTEN-FREE EGG DOUGH

For a long time I tried (and failed) to make a gluten-free pasta that resulted in a smooth, well-flavoured dough. This is the recipe I'm finally happy with, using chickpea (gram) flour. It works best with ribbon pastas – *tagliatelle*, *taglierini* and *pappardelle*. Making filled pasta with it is challenging, as without gluten the dough is less pliable and can crumble if you overwork it. I can't imagine life without pasta, so I'm really happy to be able to offer a gluten-free version.

300g/3¼ cups chickpea (gram) flour
3 eggs

**MAKES 400G/14OZ.
ENOUGH TO SERVE 4**

Place the flour on a clean work surface or board and shape it into a mound. Make a well in the centre and crack the eggs into the middle.

Using a fork, break the egg yolks and start to gently whisk them. Draw in the flour a little at a time and continue to mix with the fork.

When everything starts to come together, use your hands to knead the dough for 8–10 minutes until smooth. Use the heel of one hand to push the dough away from you, and use your other hand to turn it 90 degrees after each knead – you will soon develop a lovely rhythm.

When the dough is smooth, form it into a flat disc (this will be much easier to roll out later). Wrap it tightly in clingfilm (plastic wrap) and rest in the fridge for at least 30 minutes.

USING A FOOD PROCESSOR
You can also make pasta dough in a food processor – follow the method given on page 26.

VEGAN SEMOLINA DOUGH

This eggless dough is made from fine semolina, a type of flour ground from durum wheat. When it is cooked it has more bite than the softer egg pasta, and it also takes longer to cook – around 5–6 minutes instead of 2 minutes. I love eating this pasta with rich sauces like slow-cooked tomato, *cacio e pepe* (page 114) or ragù.

280g/1⅔ cups fine semolina
130g/4½oz warm water

**MAKES 400G/14OZ.
ENOUGH TO SERVE 4**

Place the semolina in a large mixing bowl, add a pinch of salt and pour in the warm water.

Combine with a fork – it will soon look like a crumble mix – and start to form the dough into a loose ball with your hands.

As soon as the dough has come together well, turn it onto a board or clean work surface and knead until it is elastic and smooth – this will take about 10–15 minutes. Use the heel of one hand to push the dough away from you, and use your other hand to turn it 90 degrees after each knead – you will soon develop a lovely rhythm.

Now form the dough into a flat disc (this will be much easier to roll out later). Wrap it tightly in clingfilm (plastic wrap) and rest in the fridge for at least 30 minutes.

USING A STAND MIXER
You can make this dough in a stand mixer with a dough hook attachment. Simply place the ingredients in the mixer bowl, start on a slow speed and mix steadily until the dough is formed. Tip onto a work surface, flatten into a disc and wrap in clingfilm (plastic wrap), as above.

SPINACH EGG DOUGH

This vibrant green dough gives a whole new meaning to the instruction 'eat your greens'! Use by itself or combine it with the rich egg dough (page 27) to make a colourful striped pasta (page 44). Once the spinach is combined into the dough you won't notice the taste, but I like eating it with garlicky sautéed spinach and other green veg anyway.

150g/5½oz spinach leaves, washed
1 egg, plus 1 egg yolk
250g/2 cups Italian 00 flour

**MAKES 400G/14OZ.
ENOUGH TO SERVE 4**

Bring a pan of water to the boil and blanch the spinach for 30–45 seconds, then tip into a colander to drain and rinse immediately under cold running water. When it's cool enough to handle, squeeze the spinach until you've removed almost all of the moisture.

Transfer the spinach to a blender with the whole egg, and blend until it forms a loose purée – you should get about 100–110g/3½–4oz.

Mound the flour on a clean work surface or board and create a well in the centre. Pour the spinach purée into the middle and add the egg yolk. Start mixing the dough, using a fork to draw in a little bit of flour at a time.

When the dough starts to come together, use your hands to knead for 8–10 minutes until smooth. Use the heel of one hand to push the dough away from you, and use the other to turn it 90 degrees after each knead – you will soon develop a rhythm.

When the dough is smooth, form it into a flat disc (this will be much easier to roll out later). Wrap it tightly in clingfilm (plastic wrap) and rest in the fridge for at least 30 minutes, or ideally overnight.

USING A FOOD PROCESSOR

Make the spinach pureé as above, then transfer to a bowl, add the extra egg yolk and beat gently together to combine.

Place the flour in the processor bowl and secure the lid. Start the machine, then pour the spinach purée into the funnel.

Mix for 30 seconds, until the dough has the consistency of fine breadcrumbs.

Tip onto a board or into a bowl and use your hands to bring the mixture together to form a neat disc. Wrap the dough tightly in clingfilm (plastic wrap) and refrigerate, as above.

VEGAN SPINACH DOUGH

This is a good way of introducing reluctant kids (or adults) to spinach, as there's a slightly bitter flavour to this leafy green that some people don't always like, but you won't taste it here at all. Try making this pasta with children, as it's a vivid green (like Rex, the sensitive dinosaur in *Toy Story*) and they can eat it with pesto – a perfect teatime combination.

250–300g/9–10½oz spinach, washed
150g/5½oz water
300g/1¾ cups fine semolina

**MAKES 400G/14OZ.
ENOUGH TO SERVE 4**

Bring a pan of water to the boil and blanch the spinach for 30–45 seconds, then tip it into a colander to drain and rinse immediately under cold running water. When it's cool enough to handle, squeeze the spinach until you've removed almost all of the moisture.

Place the spinach in a blender, add the water and blend for a minute until you have a lovely green liquid.

Transfer the liquid to a sieve placed over a medium bowl, then leave to sit for 5 minutes until all the liquid has drained into the bowl. You should end up with 140–150g/5–5½oz of spinach liquid. You do need to weigh it, and if you need more liquid, top it up with water. Discard the remaining spinach pulp – it can go in your compost bin.

Add the semolina and a pinch of salt to a large mixing bowl, then pour the spinach liquid all over it. Combine with a fork a little at a time – it will soon look like a crumble mix – then form it into a loose ball with your hands.

Tip the dough onto a clean work surface or board and knead it for 10 minutes, or until the dough feels elastic and smooth. Use the heel of one hand to push the dough away from you, and use your other hand to turn it 90 degrees after each knead.

Now form the dough into a flat disc (this will be much easier to roll out later). Wrap it tightly in clingfilm (plastic wrap) and rest in the fridge for at least 30 minutes.

USING A STAND MIXER
You can make this dough in a stand mixer with a dough hook attachment. Simply place the ingredients in the mixer bowl, start on a slow speed and mix steadily until the dough is formed. Tip onto a work surface and flatten into a disc. Wrap in clingfilm (plastic wrap) and refrigerate, as above.

BEETROOT EGG DOUGH

This will create a bright, beetroot (beet) red dough that I use to make a stripy dough for filled pasta (page 44). I don't really use it on its own for ribbon pastas like *tagliatelle*, *taglierini* or *pappardelle* as it goes a bit pink when you cook it, but this may go down well with certain small people who are fans of the colour!

200g/7oz raw dark red beetroot (beets), peeled and chopped into small pieces
60g/2¼oz water
1 egg, plus 2 egg yolks
250g/2 cups Italian 00 flour

MAKE 400G/14OZ.
ENOUGH TO SERVE 4

Put the beetroot (beets) into a blender and add the water, then blend to a purée. Add a little more water if you need to, but the key is to achieve a purée by adding as little liquid as possible.

Strain the purée through a sieve but don't press it – leave it to drip for 5 minutes. You will soon have a bowlful of bright-red liquid.

Weigh out 40g/1½oz of the liquid into a bowl (the pulp left in the strainer can be added to the compost). Crack in the whole egg, add the 2 egg yolks and mix together with a fork.

Mound up the flour on a clean work surface or board and create a well in the centre. Pour the beetroot (beet) and egg mixture into the middle and start mixing the dough, using a fork to draw in a little bit of flour at a time.

When everything starts to come together, use your hands to knead the dough for 8–10 minutes until smooth. Use the heel of one hand to push the dough away from you, and use your other hand to turn it 90 degrees after each knead.

When the dough is smooth, form it into a flat disc (easier to roll out later). Wrap it tightly in clingfilm (plastic wrap) and place in the fridge for at least 30 minutes, or ideally overnight.

USING A FOOD PROCESSOR
Make the beetroot (beet) and egg mixture as above.

Place the flour in the processor bowl and secure the lid. Start the machine, then pour the beetroot (beet) and egg mixture into the funnel.

Mix for 30 seconds, until the dough has the consistency of fine breadcrumbs.

Tip onto a board or into a bowl, and use your hands to bring the mixture together to form a neat disc. Wrap the dough in clingfilm (plastic wrap) and refrigerate, as above.

VEGAN BEETROOT DOUGH

This is a really vibrant, bright-red dough because there is no egg to tone down the colour of the beetroot. Make sure you choose the old-fashioned purple beetroot so that you get the brightest possible colour in your pasta.

500g/1lb 2oz raw dark red beetroot (beets), peeled and chopped
140–150g/5½–5¾oz water
300g/10½oz fine semolina

MAKES 400/14OZ.
ENOUGH TO SERVE 4

Place the beetroot into a blender and add 140g/5½oz water, then blend to a purée. Add a little more water if you need to, but the key is to achieve a purée by adding as little liquid as possible.

Strain the purée through a sieve placed over a bowl, but don't press it, just leave it to drip for 5 minutes. You will soon have a bowl of beautiful red liquid. You should get 150g/5¾oz of liquid – you do need to weigh it, and if you need more liquid, top it up with water. The bits left in the strainer can go in the compost bin.

Add the semolina and a pinch of salt to a large mixing bowl, then pour the beetroot liquid all over it. Combine with a fork a little at a time – it will soon look like a crumble mix – then form it into a loose ball with your hands.

Tip the dough onto a clean work surface or board and knead it for 10 minutes, or until the dough feels elastic and smooth. Use the heel of your hand to push the dough away from you, and use your other hand to turn it 90 degrees after each knead – you will soon develop a lovely rhythm.

Now form the dough into a flat disc (this will be much easier to roll out later). Wrap it tightly in baking parchment or clingfilm (plastic wrap) and rest in the fridge for 30 minutes.

USING A STAND MIXER
You can make this dough in a stand mixer with a dough hook attachment. Simply place the ingredients in the mixer bowl, start on a slow speed and mix steadily until the dough is formed. Tip onto a work surface, flatten into a disc and wrap in clingfilm (plastic wrap), as above.

SQUID INK EGG DOUGH

This inky dough carries a strong flavour of the sea; the taste is more noticeable than in either the spinach or beetroot (beet) pasta, which don't really taste of the vegetables at all. I usually pair this with fish-based pastas, such as prawn *cappelletti* or crab *taglierini*. Try making striped pasta with squid ink pasta and rich egg dough (page 27) – it's a lot of fun and creates a dramatic contrast on the plate. You can buy squid ink at a good fishmonger's, at a supermarket fish counter or at specialist online grocery stores.

2 eggs, plus 2 egg yolks
40g/1½oz squid ink
320g/2½ cups Italian 00 flour

**MAKES 400G/14OZ.
ENOUGH TO SERVE 4**

Mix together the eggs, egg yolks and squid ink in a small bowl, making sure the whole mixture becomes black – you shouldn't see any streaks of yellow or orange yolk at all.

Place the flour on a clean work surface or board and pile it into a mound. Make a well in the centre and pour the egg and ink mixture into it. Using a fork, start mixing the dough, drawing in a little bit of flour at a time.

When everything starts to come together, use your hands to knead the dough for 8–10 minutes until smooth. Use the heel of one hand to push the dough away from you, and use your other hand to turn it 90 degrees after each knead – you will soon develop a lovely rhythm.

When the dough is smooth, form it into a flat disc (this will be much easier to roll out later). Wrap it tightly in clingfilm (plastic wrap) and place in the fridge for at least 30 minutes, or ideally overnight. This allows the dough to rest and makes it easier to roll out and shape.

USING A FOOD PROCESSOR
Make the egg and ink mixture as above.

Place the flour in the processor bowl and secure the lid. Start the machine, then pour the egg and ink mixture into the funnel.

Mix for 30 seconds, until the dough has the consistency of fine breadcrumbs.

Tip onto a board or into a bowl, and use your hands to bring the mixture together to form a neat disc.

Wrap the dough in clingfilm (plastic wrap) and rest in the fridge for a minimum of 30 minutes, or ideally overnight.

ROLLING & SHAPING PASTA

Now you can make pasta dough, it's time to start (rocking &) rolling.

Tagliatelle, *taglierini* and *pappardelle* are the easiest shapes to make, so it's a good idea to start with these. Kids seem to love both making and eating all of them, partly because it's so much fun turning the handle of the pasta machine and seeing the dough flatten and grow, but also for the fun of twirling long ribbons of pasta around a fork. It can get messy, so just don't wear your favourite white t-shirt.

Of the filled pasta shapes, *ravioli* is definitely the easiest, while *agnolotti del plin* and *culurgiones* are a bit more fiddly. OK, they're a *lot* more fiddly, but you will soon get the knack if you practise a few times, and they are incredibly satisfying shapes to make – not to mention being some of my favourites to eat.

You can also make two-toned pasta (page 44) using either the classic or rich egg dough (pages 26 and 27) in combination with the black squid, green spinach or beetroot (beet) red doughs (pages 36, 32, and 34). For these, use 200g/7oz or half a quantity of each dough. Once you have learned this technique, you will be able to create some colourful pasta dishes to wow your dinner guests.

A FEW NOTES ON ROLLING PASTA

The widest setting on my pasta machine is 0, so the settings I have used in this book are based on this. If your machine settings are reversed (i.e. if 0 is the thinnest setting on your machine), reverse the setting numbers accordingly throughout.

If possible, always take your dough out of the fridge 30 minutes before shaping because it's much easier to roll it at room temperature.

It's generally easiest to work with a quarter of the dough at a time (so, in 100g/3½oz portions). This prevents the dough drying out as you work, and you won't need to rush to finish rolling. Leave the rest of the dough wrapped in clingfilm (plastic wrap) or under a damp tea (dish) towel until you need it.

Prepare a tray or baking sheet lightly dusted with coarse semolina, ready for your finished pasta shapes, and dust the pasta with more semolina as you lay it out. This is to prevent it sticking together.

You should allow your pasta to dry for around 30 minutes or so before cooking, but if you are making it any more than an hour ahead, wrap the whole tray in clingfilm (plastic wrap) to prevent it from drying out too much.

Don't throw away any leftover scraps of pasta after shaping – use them as *maltagliati* for *minestrone* (page 150). Simply freeze in a container or, if you prefer, freeze flat on a tray and transfer to a freezer container later.

You can re-use any semolina that is left on the work surface once you've finished. It's best to pick out any stray slivers of pasta first, then just keep the semolina in a container for the next time you're making pasta.

ROLLING OUT PASTA DOUGH

This is the rolling technique you'll need to refer to when you make any of the recipes in this book. Once you've done it a few times, you'll become increasingly confident, and will soon be familiar with the settings on your machine. The machine setting number for each pasta shape is included in the method, but just check back here if you're happier being guided step-by-step.

If the pasta is sticky and proves difficult to roll out, dust it gently with Italian 00 flour (the same flour you used to make the dough). Pat it lightly over the surface so that the dough just absorbs the flour, and you should be able to continue.

Cut roughly a quarter from your disc of pasta dough, then flatten it a little and guide it through the widest setting on your pasta machine twice (on my machine this is 0).

Move to the next widest setting (on my machine this is 1), then take the dough through this setting twice.

Now click back to the widest setting. Fold the dough in half from end to end, flatten it slightly and roll it through the machine twice.

Click to the next widest setting (you're now on 1 again). Roll it through the machine twice.

Then continue to guide the dough twice through each thickness setting. If you are making long ribbon pastas – *tagliatelle*, *taglierini*, *pappardelle* or *garganelli* – stop rolling at setting 7. If you are making filled pastas such as *ravioli*, *tortellini* or *cappelletti*, you want the dough to be finer, so stop rolling on setting 8.

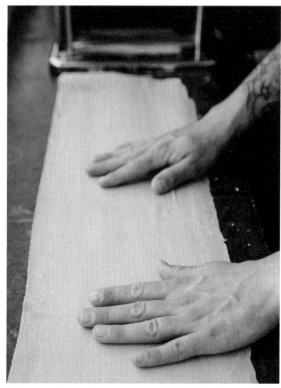

MULTI-COLOURED PASTA

When I post images of my multi-coloured pasta shapes on social media, I always get a lot of great comments as well as questions about how I do it. I enjoy playing around with the different types of dough and filling, and it has become another way of engaging people in conversations about making pasta and encouraging them to try it at home.

It's really fun to make coloured pastas, even if you just make a single-coloured dough, but when you start to blend two or more, you'll soon be hooked. So once you're really confident about making classic fresh egg pasta at home, why not play around with stripes and patterns?

Some of my recipes suggest using two separate pasta doughs because it can look really special to have a bowl of mixed *tagliatelle* using spinach and classic egg dough, for example. But generally, the striped doughs are best used for filled pastas, where you can really complement the shapes you make.

I'm going to show you three ways to make multi-coloured pasta sheets with egg pasta doughs. The first method is the most technical, but it wastes less dough and will give you amazing stripes on both sides. Once you've got the hang of it, this is the best technique to use to make three-, four- or even five-coloured striped doughs.

The second is really simple and fun, but the stripes will only show on one side of the sheet. The third follows the same principles, but for making polka-dot pasta.

So, let's get started.

TWO-SIDED STRIPES

**200g/7oz classic or rich egg dough
(pages 26 and 27)
200g/7oz any coloured egg dough
(pages 32, 34 and 36)**

Take one quarter of the classic or rich egg dough. (Weigh it out carefully as you need exact quantities to create an even finish.) Flatten the dough to make it easier to start rolling. Roll the dough through the widest setting of your pasta machine (0 on mine). Roll it again through the same setting, tidying the edges to make an even rectangle. If the sides are still wavy, fold the dough lengthways and roll again. When you have a neat rectangle, cover with a damp tea (dish) towel or clingfilm (plastic wrap) and set aside.

Repeat the above with a weighed quarter of the coloured dough.

Using a sharp knife, cut both doughs lengthways into 1cm/½in wide strips. Working quickly, spread out a sheet of baking parchment and lay alternate colours of dough side by side. The strips should just touch and not overlap – you will need to nudge them to lie snugly together. Roll back and forth with a rolling pin, pressing gently so that the edges of the stripes connect to one another.

Carefully and slowly peel the sheet off the baking parchment. You may need to lift it from beneath with the blade of a large knife. Pass it through the pasta machine on the second widest setting, working very slowly.

Pass the dough twice more through each setting, finishing on 7 or 8 (stop at 7 if you're happy with the consistency).

Trim the ends to make neat edges and you are ready to shape your pasta!

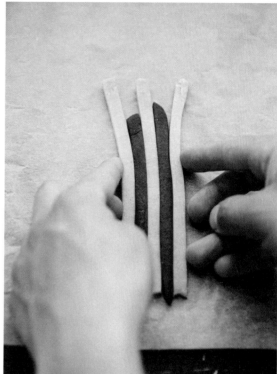

ONE-SIDE-ONLY STRIPES

**200g/7oz classic or rich egg dough
(pages 26 and 27)**
**200g/7oz any coloured egg dough
(pages 32, 34 and 36)**

Cut roughly one quarter from your disc of classic or rich egg dough, then flatten it a little and guide it twice through the widest setting on your pasta machine (0 on mine). Move to the next widest setting, then take the dough through twice. Fold the dough in half from end to end, flatten it slightly and roll through the machine twice again on the widest setting, then guide the dough twice through each subsequent setting. For filled pasta such as *ravioli*, *tortellini* or *cappelletti*, you want a fine, pliable dough, so stop rolling on setting 8.

Lay out the pasta on a work surface or table. Cover with a damp dish towel or clingfilm (plastic wrap). Repeat the above process with a quarter of the coloured dough.

Lay the coloured sheet flat on the table and, using a sharp knife, cut strips of around 1cm/½in wide across the width of the dough. I use a metal ruler to keep the strips straight. Now arrange the coloured strips across the width of the egg dough sheet, laying them 1cm/½in apart for nice, even stripes, or play around with alternate thick or thin stripes, diagonals or chequerboard patterns. Some of the coloured strips may overhang the edges of the sheet of egg dough, so trim to tidy up.

Using a rolling pin, roll gently over the whole sheet to connect the coloured stripes to the egg dough sheet beneath.

Finally, guide the dough through the pasta machine again on setting 8. This will give you the finished, striped sheet of dough.

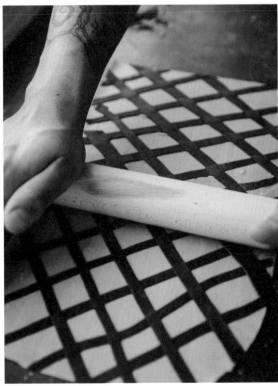

POLKA DOT

▼▼▼▼▼▼▼▼▼▼▼▼▼▼▼▼▼▼▼▼▼▼▼

**200g/7oz classic or rich egg dough
(pages 26 and 27)
200g/7oz any coloured egg dough
(pages 32, 34 and 36)**

Cut roughly one quarter from your disc of classic or rich egg dough, then flatten it a little and guide it twice through the widest setting on your pasta machine (0 on mine). Move to the next widest setting, then take the dough through twice. Fold the dough in half from end to end, flatten it slightly and roll through the machine twice again on the widest setting, then guide the dough twice through each subsequent setting. For filled pasta such as *ravioli*, *tortellini* or *cappelletti*, you want a fine, pliable dough, so stop rolling on setting 8.

Lay out the pasta on a work surface or table. Cover with a damp dish towel or clingfilm (plastic wrap).

Repeat the above process with a quarter of the coloured dough.

Lay the coloured sheet flat on the table and, using a small ring cutter, cut circles out of your dough.

Now arrange the coloured circles across the width of the egg dough sheet, evenly spaced apart. Play around with multiple colours of dough if you like.

Using a rolling pin, roll gently over the whole sheet to connect the coloured dots to the egg dough sheet beneath.

Finally, guide the dough through the pasta machine again on setting 8. This will give you the finished, polka dot sheet of dough.

THE SHAPES
& RECIPES

PAPPARDELLE

If you're used to buying dried *pappardelle* you're probably familiar with the long, flat strands about the width of your thumb, but if you make it fresh it's nice to be generous and make really wide strands. This pasta is often served with rich, meaty sauces, making it a winter favourite, and I like to pair it with autumnal (fall) ingredients like pumpkin, earthy mushrooms and cavolo nero, a cabbage that always seems to taste sweeter after the first frosts.

Start with half the dough, keeping the other half tightly wrapped, and prepare a tray or baking sheet dusted with coarse semolina, ready to lay out your finished pasta.

Following the method on page 40, roll out your pasta dough, stopping at setting 7.

Decide what length you want the *pappardelle* ribbons and cut your dough to that length – maybe start with 15–20cm/6–8in long.

Dust each pasta sheet with semolina once you've cut it, then carefully stack the generously dusted sheets on top of one another. The aim is to produce a tidy pile, like a neat pack of playing cards.

When you've finished rolling the first half of the dough, gently fold the stack of sheets in half widthways and turn the fold towards you.

Using a sharp knife, cut the sheets into ribbons about 3cm/1¼in wide.

Gently lift each stack of ribbons and shake off the semolina (it's ok if some clings to the strands). Lay the ribbons in neat piles or folds on your tray, cover with clingfilm (plastic wrap), then roll out the other half of the dough. If you are cutting the pasta more than an hour ahead of cooking, cover the whole tray with clingfilm to keep it airtight.

PAPPARDELLE WITH CAVOLO NERO & BURRATA

Cavolo nero (black cabbage or Tuscan kale) makes for a healthy, fresh pasta sauce full of vitamins and iron. The addition of creamy burrata complements the grassy flavour of the kale and makes this dish really special.

400g/14oz egg *pappardelle* (page 54)

1 whole small garlic bulb
150g/5½oz cavolo nero (about 10 whole leaves)
juice of ½ small lemon
100ml/7 tablespoons olive oil, plus extra for drizzling
20g/¾oz Parmesan or pecorino, grated
2 balls of burrata, halved

SERVES 4

Preheat the oven to 180°C fan/400°F/gas mark 6.

Cut 1cm/½in off the top of the garlic bulb so the cloves are exposed. Wrap the whole garlic in foil and twist the top closed, then roast for 25 minutes until it's soft.

Remove and discard the stalks from the cavolo nero and wash the stripped leaves under cold water. Bring a large pan of water to the boil before adding salt. Blanch the leaves for 30 seconds, then immediately transfer them to a bowl of cold water (this will help keep their green colour). Set aside the pan of salted water to cook the pasta in.

Press the cavolo nero leaves to remove as much water as you can, and put them into a food processor or blender. Add the lemon juice. Squeeze the roasted garlic cloves out of their skins and add them to the processor or blender. Start blending the ingredients together, slowly adding the olive oil as you go, and finishing with the Parmesan.

Bring the pan of salted water back to the boil and cook the *pappardelle* for 1½–2 minutes. At the same time, pour the cavolo nero sauce into a large saucepan on a low heat. When the pasta is cooked, add it to the sauce with a ladleful (or two) of pasta water. Combine together using tongs or simply toss it. Check the seasoning – it will need salt – and the sauce might need to be loosened with more pasta water.

Divide between bowls. Place half a ball of burrata on top of each serving, drizzle with olive oil and add a twist of black pepper.

VEGAN OPTION

Use *chitarra* made with vegan dough (page 82) instead of the egg *pappardelle*.

Use 20g/¾oz nutritional yeast instead of the Parmesan.

Finish with *pangrattato* (page 153) instead of burrata.

PAPPARDELLE WITH MUSHROOM & SEAWEED

One day I received a parcel from my friend Yuichi in Japan, containing lots of beautifully wrapped Japanese ingredients – a few types of seaweed, bonito flakes, yuzu chilli paste and wasabi powder. I started to experiment with fusing Japanese cuisines with pasta (which originated in Asia anyway). Here, the seaweed gives the sauce texture and the shiitake mushrooms have a meaty, umami flavour, but you can use any mushroom you like. Seaweed can be overpowering, so I only use a little, adding mascarpone to soften it slightly. If you do add egg yolks at the end it will give a real wow factor to the dish, but it will still taste special without.

400g/14oz egg *pappardelle*
 (page 54)

45ml/3 tablespoons olive oil
3 garlic cloves, finely chopped
300g/10½oz fresh shiitake (or
 other meaty) mushrooms,
 roughly chopped
100g/3½oz mascarpone
juice of 1 lemon
3 teaspoons dried seaweed
4 egg yolks, to serve (optional)
Parmesan, to serve (optional)

SERVES 4

Heat the olive oil in a large saucepan, add the garlic and fry for 1 minute on a medium heat until just golden. Add the mushrooms and continue cooking for 5 minutes, stirring from time to time. Season with salt and pepper and remove from the heat.

If you are going to finish the dish with egg yolks, now is the time to crack and separate the eggs; use the whites in other dishes.

Next, cook the *pappardelle* in a large pan of boiling salted water – this should take about 1½–2 minutes. Drain, but keep a jugful of the cooking water.

Put the mushroom pan back on the heat, add the mascarpone and a ladleful of pasta cooking water, then add the drained pasta and lemon juice. Cook on a medium heat until the sauce is creamy, then scatter the seaweed on top and toss everything together, or use tongs to combine it all. If the sauce looks dry, add some more cooking water and check the seasoning.

Divide the pasta between four plates, then if you're finishing with a raw egg yolk, place one on top of each plate before serving, when everything is still hot. It's fun to split the egg yolk with your fork and mix it into the sauce. Put a chunk of Parmesan and the grater in the middle of the table so people can help themselves.

VEGAN OPTION

Use a dried eggless pasta (*linguine* or *spaghetti*) instead of the egg *pappardelle*.

Use oat cream instead of mascarpone.

Finish the dish with nutritional yeast or *pangrattato* (page 153) instead of Parmesan and an egg yolk.

CHICKEN LIVER & LEEK PAPPARDELLE

We ate chicken livers at least once a week when I was growing up. It's not really a happy food memory, as they were usually overcooked, but my grandmother said they were full of vitamins and iron and would make me grow up big and strong. Luckily I still like them, and cooked well, seared on the outside but still lovely and pink inside, there's nothing better. Track down good-quality livers either at the butcher's or at a farmers' market, preferably organic – it's definitely worth the money.

400g/14oz egg *pappardelle*
  (page 54)

500g/1lb 2oz chicken livers
30ml/2 tablespoons olive oil
4 shallots (approx. 300g/10½oz),
  finely diced
40g/1½oz butter
10 sage leaves, chopped
1 medium leek, quartered
  lengthways and sliced into
  3–4cm/1¼ –1½in pieces
100ml/7 tablespoons white wine
100ml/7 tablespoons marsala
  (or white wine)
handful of parsley, chopped, to serve
Parmesan, grated, to serve

SERVES 4

First, clean the chicken livers, removing any white sinew, and place into a mixing bowl. Season the livers with a few twists of salt and fresh black pepper and coat with the olive oil.

In a pan over a low heat, gently sweat the shallots in half of the butter until soft and translucent (about 10 minutes). Add the sage leaves, then tip out into a bowl and set aside.

Using the same pan, fry the leeks in the remaining butter for 7–8 minutes until soft, pour over the white wine and let this bubble for 5 minutes to reduce. Add to the bowl of shallots.

Set the pan back on a high heat and fry the chicken livers for 2–3 minutes until they are seared but still rosy inside. Transfer the livers to a bowl and set aside to cool. Still on a high heat, add the marsala to the pan, stirring with a wooden spoon to loosen any bits of veg sticking to the base. The liquid will absorb all the delicious flavours slightly burned into the pan, which you really don't want to waste. Remove from the heat.

Roughly chop the chicken livers and combine with the shallots and leeks in the pan with the marsala.

Bring a large pan of water to the boil before adding salt, then drop in the *pappardelle* and cook for 1½–2 minutes.

Gently heat through the liver sauce and, using tongs, lift the *pappardelle* into the pan, together with a good splash of the pasta cooking water. Sprinkle over the parsley, check for seasoning, and serve with a generous grating of Parmesan.

PAPPARDELLE WITH CREAMY PUMPKIN SAUCE

Pumpkins and squashes are so versatile and I can never resist buying them when I see them piled up in colourful pyramids at the local market in autumn (fall). You can use them in soups, curries and sauces, or simply roast them with cumin and chilli flakes or a handful of herbs. You can use pretty much any pumpkin or squash in this recipe – add a pinch of cinnamon and nutmeg if you like, but I like the earthy flavour of fresh sage leaves which contrasts with the sweet pumpkin.

400g/14oz egg *pappardelle* (page 54)

500g/1lb 2oz pumpkin or squash, peeled, deseeded and chopped into medium-sized cubes
3 garlic cloves, in their skins
100ml/7 tablespoons warm water
30ml/2 tablespoons olive oil, plus extra for roasting
½ teaspoon sea salt
2 tablespoons mascarpone
15–20 fresh sage leaves
20g/¾oz Parmesan, grated, plus extra to serve

SERVES 4

Preheat the oven to 175°C fan/375°F/gas mark 5 and line a roasting tin with baking parchment.

Put the pumpkin cubes and garlic cloves in a roasting tin, drizzle with olive oil, sprinkle with sea salt and turn everything together with your hands to make sure it's well coated with oil. Roast for 30–40 minutes until soft. Remove from the oven and allow to cool.

Squeeze the roasted garlic cloves out of their skins into a food processor or blender, adding the roasted pumpkin, warm water, olive oil and fine salt. Blend everything together to make a creamy sauce, then transfer to a large saucepan and set it over a really low heat.

Now you are ready to cook your *pappardelle*. Drop the pasta into a large pan of boiling salted water and cook for 1½–2 minutes, then transfer the pasta to the sauce using tongs.

Add half a ladleful of the pasta cooking water, the mascarpone and the sage leaves, and toss to combine everything together. Scatter over the Parmesan, grind in some black pepper, mix once again and finally check the seasoning. Serve with a bowl of grated Parmesan so that everyone can help themselves to more.

VEGAN OPTION

Use a dried eggless pasta (*linguine* or *spaghetti*) instead of the egg *pappardelle*.

Use almond cream or almond milk instead of mascarpone.

Finish with *pangrattato* (page 153) instead of Parmesan.

OX TAIL RAGÙ WITH PAPPARDELLE

This beef ragù is based on one of the most memorable pasta sauces I've ever eaten. It was cooked by Florence Knight, the head chef at Polpetto in Soho, who ran the best, friendliest kitchen I've ever worked in. You can use ox cheeks or even diced beef (you only need 800g/1lb 12oz if the beef is without the bone), but I use ox tail, which is classic *cucina povera* or 'peasant food' – using inexpensive, disregarded ingredients, often slow-cooked in soups and stews to bring out their amazing flavour. Ox tail is quite fatty, and although many people are afraid of fat, where there's fat, there's flavour. I sometimes add bone marrow to this mix for that reason. This recipe makes more ragù than you'll need for four people – you can freeze the rest for use next time.

400g/14oz egg *pappardelle*
   (page 54)

1.2kg/2lb 11oz ox tail pieces
45ml/3 tablespoons olive oil
1 large onion, finely diced
1 large carrot, finely diced
½ head of celery, finely diced
4 garlic cloves, finely diced
large sprig of thyme
large sprig of rosemary
3 bay leaves
350ml/1½ cups red wine
500ml/generous 2 cups beef stock
   (broth) or water
1 x 400g/14oz tin plum tomatoes
40g/1½oz olive oil or butter
burrata or grated Parmesan, to serve

SERVES 4

Preheat the oven to 150°C fan/325°F/gas mark 3.

Season the ox tail with a scattering of fine sea salt and freshly ground black pepper. Set a large frying pan on a medium heat, add 30ml/2 tablespoons of the olive oil and gently brown off the sides of the ox tail. Once it has a nice rich colour, remove from the heat and lift the meat into a casserole dish (preferably one with a lid) that can be used on the hob.

Using the same frying pan, add the remaining olive oil along with the onion, carrot and celery and sweat them down for at least 20 minutes, until very soft and sweet (this mixture is called *soffritto* in Italian, the classic base for so many flavourful soups and sauces). Add the garlic and fry for a further 2 minutes.

Add the *soffritto* to the casserole dish, along with the herbs, red wine, beef stock (broth) or water and the tomatoes, and bring to a simmer. Make sure the meat is covered with liquid and, if necessary, top up with a little water.

Cover the casserole dish with a lid or wrap it tightly with foil and cook in the oven for 4 hours or until the meat is very tender. It's a good idea to check the dish halfway through and top up with water if it looks a little dry.

When the ragù is cooked, remove all the ox tail pieces to a bowl and set aside to cool. Pick out the herbs and discard them. Once cool enough, check for stray bones, then use a hand blender or food processor to blitz the liquid and vegetables to create a rich-coloured sauce. Return the mixture to the casserole dish.

When the ox tail is cool enough to handle, pull all the meat from the bone and add to the sauce, breaking up any large pieces of meat. Discard the bones and fat. Place the sauce on a low heat, stir well to combine, then leave to simmer gently for 20 minutes. Check for seasoning. At this point, I transfer 320g/11½oz of the ragù to a separate saucepan and set aside the rest for freezing.

Bring a large pan of water to the boil before adding salt, and cook the *pappardelle* for 1½–2 minutes.

Using tongs, transfer the pasta to the sauce with a ladleful of the cooking water and the olive oil or butter. Toss or gently mix the pasta and ragù together, then transfer to a large, warmed serving bowl to let people help themselves. If you like, serve with a plate of burrata and a green salad on the side, or simply cover in a snowstorm of Parmesan.

TAGLIATELLE

▼▼▼▼▼▼▼▼▼▼▼▼▼▼▼▼▼▼▼▼▼▼▼▼▼

The name of this pasta derives from the word *tagliere*, which means 'to cut' in Italian. We roll first, then we cut – easy-peasy. Your pasta machine should come with an attachment to cut *tagliatelle*.

Start with half the dough, leaving the other half wrapped, and have ready a tray or baking sheet dusted with coarse semolina. Following the method on page 40, roll out your pasta dough, stopping at setting 7, then cut the sheets into 25cm/10in lengths.

Attach the pasta cutter to your machine and guide the sheets through on the *tagliatelle* setting.

Dust the cut pasta with semolina and either lay it flat or lift it by the centre of the strands and curl it into individual nests on the tray. Leave to one side for 30 minutes, so that the pasta dries slightly before cooking. If you are shaping the *tagliatelli* more than an hour ahead of cooking, cover the whole tray with clingfilm (plastic wrap) so it is airtight.

STRIPED TAGLIATELLE WITH ARTICHOKES & CAPERS

This sauce is all about the perfect balance of flavours – acid from the lemon, saltiness from the capers, a touch of sourness in the artichokes and a bit of heat from the red chillies. This dish takes me back to the Mediterranean countryside, with fields full of artichokes and capers, drinking good wine on a farm. Classic Italian flavours – quick and simple. What more could you want?

You can of course make this with classic egg dough, but it's always fun to play with the stripy dough. If you do, then simply make half the quantity of the egg dough and half of the coloured dough (I like to use spinach dough here, see page 32) to give you 400g/14oz in total.

400g/14oz striped egg *tagliatelle* (page 64)

45ml/3 tablespoons olive oil
2 red chillies, deseeded and finely chopped
4 garlic cloves, finely chopped
zest of 1 lemon and juice of ½ lemon
40g/⅓ cup capers
250g/9oz marinated artichokes from a jar, chopped
bunch of parsley, finely chopped
Parmesan or pecorino, to serve

SERVES 4

Heat the olive oil in a large saucepan on a low–medium heat and fry the chillies and garlic for 2–3 minutes until fragrant. Add the lemon zest, capers, artichokes and 50ml/3½ tablespoons of water and cook for a further 5 minutes, stirring occasionally.

Meanwhile, bring a large pan of water to the boil before adding salt. Drop the *tagliatelle* into the water and cook for 1½–2 minutes.

Transfer the cooked pasta to the sauce and mix well, then scatter the parsley all over the pasta and toss it again. Grind over black paper, add the lemon juice, then check the seasoning – remember that the capers are really salty, but you can always add an extra pinch of salt if you feel it needs it.

Divide between four plates, scattering some Parmesan or pecorino on top.

VEGAN OPTION
Use *malloreddus* or *capunti* (pages 106 and 116) instead of the egg *tagliatelle*.

Finish with *pangrattato* (page 153) or nutritional yeast instead of Parmesan or pecorino.

FENNEL, SHALLOT &
CAPER TAGLIATELLE

This dish reminds me of being in my garden, picking wild fennel and crushing it in my hand – the soft aniseed scent is so fragrant. Mixed with the sweetness of shallots, thyme and salty capers for crunch, this dish makes the most of its fresh flavour – I hope you will love it too.

400g/14oz egg *tagliatelle*
(page 64)

60ml/4 tablespoons olive oil
3 garlic cloves, thinly sliced
2 shallots, finely sliced lengthwise
1 large fennel bulb (approx.
400g/14oz), thinly sliced
1 tablespoon capers, chopped
1 tablespoon thyme leaves
juice of ½ lemon
Parmesan or pecorino, grated,
to serve

SERVES 4

Heat the olive oil in a large pan, then fry the garlic for 30 seconds until fragrant. Add the sliced shallots and fennel and cook on a low heat for 10–15 minutes until they are soft and just turning golden, then add the capers, thyme and lemon juice and stir through. Continue cooking on a low heat, stirring every few minutes, to let all the flavours combine.

Bring a large pan of water to the boil before adding salt, then drop in the *tagliatelle* and cook for 1½–2 minutes.

Using tongs, lift the pasta into the pan of sauce, adding a ladleful of pasta cooking water to loosen the sauce. Mix to combine and season with sea salt and some freshly ground black pepper. Serve with plenty of Parmesan or pecorino, and ideally a chilled glass of dry white wine.

VEGAN OPTION

Use an eggless pasta (page 31) instead of the egg *tagliatelle*.

Finish with *pangrattato* (page 153) or nutritional yeast instead of Parmesan or pecorino.

LEMON & WALNUT TAGLIATELLE

From time to time when I see Amalfi lemons at the greengrocer's, I buy them just to have them sitting on the kitchen shelf. The queen of lemons is large, knobbly and fragrant, and you can eat the whole thing almost like an orange. If you do come across Amalfi lemons, use one to make this lovely pasta dish, to give a lemony sharpness with the crunchy bite of walnuts.

400g/14oz egg *tagliatelle*
(page 64)

1 lemon (Amalfi if possible)
1 tablespoon olive oil
60g/2¼oz butter
2 tablespoons mascarpone
60g/2¼oz Parmesan, grated
large handful of chopped walnuts,
to serve

SERVES 4

Cut the lemon in half, squeeze the juice from one half into a bowl and set aside. Slice the remaining lemon half – skin and pith included – into slivers as thin as you can make them (use a mandoline if you have one).

In a large saucepan, heat the olive oil and fry the lemon slices on both sides on a medium heat until they start to colour; they should be nice and golden, but do keep an eye on them as if they turn brown they will taste bitter. Transfer them to a bowl.

Add the butter to the pan with the mascarpone and a ladleful of water and whisk together on a low heat.

Meanwhile, bring a large pan of water to the boil before adding salt. Cook the *tagliatelle* for 1½–2 minutes, then drain and reserve a jugful of the cooking water.

Add the lemon juice and some freshly ground black pepper to the sauce, tip in the pasta and mix well. Scatter the Parmesan all over the pasta and continue cooking on a low heat until you have a glossy sauce. If the sauce needs loosening, add a ladleful of pasta cooking water. Lastly, add the fried lemon slices and season with more salt if needed.

Divide between four bowls and serve with chopped walnuts scattered over the top. *Buon appetito!*

TAGLIATELLE WITH COURGETTE, MINT & BASIL

This is a dish that reminds me of my friend, neighbour and keen gardener, Steve. I love inspecting his kitchen garden with him and sometimes I come away with some freshly picked vegetables or a handful of herbs. With such a simple recipe, good ingredients are really important and fresh local produce makes such a difference. If you can find a yellow courgette (zucchini), it will bring a splash of sunny colour to this mainly green dish, and it also seems to make it taste creamier. If you do grow your own, you can always slice and add the courgette (zucchini) flowers to the sauce at the end.

400g/14oz egg *tagliatelle*
    (page 64)

250g/9oz courgettes (zucchini) (about
    3 medium courgettes/zucchini)
bunch of mint
½ bunch basil
90ml/6 tablespoons olive oil
Parmesan, to serve

SERVES 4

Prepare the courgettes (zucchini): cut off the ends and grate the courgettes using the large holes on a box grater. Transfer to a colander or strainer, sprinkle with salt and leave for 20 minutes. After 20 minutes, gently squeeze the grated courgettes to remove any excess liquid.

Meanwhile, pick the mint and basil leaves and, leaving some small mint leaves for garnish, roughly chop the rest.

Bring a large pan of water to the boil in readiness for the pasta. At the same time, add the olive oil to a large saucepan on a medium heat, then add the grated courgette (zucchini) and a ladleful of boiling water.

Salt the boiling water for the pasta, then drop in the *tagliatelle* and cook for 1½–2 minutes. Using kitchen tongs, lift the pasta into the pan with the courgettes (zucchini). Scatter in the mint and basil and toss everything together. The sauce should just coat the pasta (you're unlikely to need to add any more of the pasta cooking water for this dish).

Check the seasoning and garnish with the remaining mint leaves. Serve with a chunk of Parmesan and let everyone help themselves.

VEGAN OPTION
Use *chitarra* made with vegan dough (page 31) instead of the egg *tagliatelle*.

Finish with *pangrattato* (page 153) instead of Parmesan for a lovely crunch.

TAGLIATELLE WITH RICH GORGONZOLA SAUCE

Saturday is market day in my town in Dorset, and this is a happy day for me. I love to visit my favourite stalls to buy fresh, locally grown produce from Springtail Farm, or to pick up cheese, olives and pasta flour at Mercato Italiano. I sometimes make this sauce when I've bought a chunk of Gorgonzola *dolce*, and I serve it with a herby green leaf salad and lemon dressing.

400g/14oz egg *tagliatelle*
   (page 64)

45ml/3 tablespoons olive oil
3 garlic cloves, sliced
2 medium onions, sliced
50ml/3½ tablespoons water
160g/5¾oz Gorgonzola
200g/7oz spinach leaves, washed
2 tablespoons mascarpone
pangrattato (page 153), to serve
   (optional)

SERVES 4

Heat the olive oil in a large saucepan and fry the garlic and onions for 10–15 minutes until they are really soft and just beginning to turn golden. Add a pinch of salt and the water and continue to cook for another 5 minutes.

Break up the Gorgonzola with your fingers and add to the pan. Cook on a low heat, stirring from time to time, until the Gorgonzola has melted into the sauce, then add the spinach and cover the pan with a lid. Cook for 2 minutes until the spinach has wilted into the sauce.

Meanwhile, bring a large pan of water to the boil before adding salt, and cook the *tagliatelle* for 1½–2 minutes.

Transfer the *tagliatelle* to the sauce using tongs, reserving a jugful of pasta water. If the sauce is too thick, add a little bit of cooking water, then stir in the mascarpone. Combine together, tossing or moving around the pasta with your tongs. When the sauce is nicely coating your pasta, you are ready to serve it. Add a twist or two of black pepper and check the seasoning.

Serve with *pangrattato* to add crunch, if you like, and a herby mixed leaf salad on the side.

SPINACH TAGLIATELLE WITH AVOCADO, PINE NUTS & BASIL

This recipe was inspired by Anna Jones, who is a fabulously inventive vegetarian cookery writer. Surprisingly, avocado brings a beautiful texture to pasta – you don't have to add much to create a lovely creamy sauce. Mashing some of the avocado and leaving the rest of it in chunks creates texture in the dish, and the pine nuts add a contrasting bite.

400g/14oz spinach egg *tagliatelle* (page 64)

45ml/3 tablespoons olive oil
2 mild red chillies, deseeded and finely chopped
4 garlic cloves, finely chopped
3 perfectly ripe avocados, peeled and roughly chopped
juice and zest of 1 lemon
bunch of basil, stems removed, leaves roughly torn
30g/¼ cup pine nuts, crushed
Parmesan or pecorino, to serve

SERVES 4

Gently heat the olive oil in a large saucepan and fry the chillies and garlic on a low heat for a couple of minutes until fragrant. Add the avocado, lemon juice and zest and cook for a couple more minutes until the avocado has absorbed the garlicky chilli oil. Use a wooden spoon to crush some of the avocados, but make sure you leave lots of chunky pieces.

Bring a large pan of water to the boil before adding salt, then drop the *tagliatelle* into the boiling water and cook for 1½–2 minutes. When the pasta is *al dente*, use tongs to transfer it to the avocado sauce. The cooking water will cling to the cooked pasta, but you will still need another ladleful (or two) to loosen the sauce.

Season with salt and freshly ground black pepper, stir in the torn basil, then toss or mix everything together using tongs or a spatula. When the pasta is nicely coated, check the seasoning again and serve, scattering the crushed pine nuts over the top of each plate. Put a chunk of Parmesan or pecorino on the table with a grater and let people help themselves.

VEGAN OPTION
Use *malloreddus* or *capunti* (pages 106 and 116) instead of the egg *tagliatelle*.

Finish with *pangrattato* (page 153) instead of Parmesan or pecorino.

TAGLIERINI

Taglierini originated in northern Italy and was said to be made from the off-cuts of filled pasta shapes, so it would have been cut by hand and the lengths would have been variable. Now you can cut it using the attachment on your pasta machine, so it's always nice and neat. I like to make these skinny ribbons quite long, and sometimes cut it in lengths of around 40cm/16in – it's nice to twirl just three or four longer strands around your fork. To start with, I suggest you cut to 25cm/10in, but it's entirely up to you.

Start with half the dough, keeping the other half tightly wrapped, and prepare a tray or baking sheet dusted with coarse semolina, ready to lay out your finished pasta.

Following the method on page 40, roll out your pasta dough, stopping at setting 7, then cut the sheets into 25cm/10in lengths.

Attach the pasta cutter to your machine and guide the sheets through on the *taglierini* setting.

Lift the cut *taglierini* and fold it into loose plaits or nests on the tray. Dust heavily with more semolina and leave to one side for 30 minutes, so that the pasta dries slightly before cooking. If you are cutting the pasta more than an hour ahead of cooking, remember to cover the whole tray with clingfilm (plastic wrap) to keep it airtight.

TAGLIERINI WITH SLOW-COOKED TOMATO SAUCE & BURRATA

When we first came to live in Dorset, our new next-door neighbours Ivan and Hanna turned out to have the most beautiful vegetable garden I had ever seen. Ivan grew an early tomato variety called Bloody Butcher, and sometimes we'd return home to find a bag full of tomatoes on our doorstep – and occasionally a bunch of sweet peas too. What could be nicer than home-grown gifts? In this recipe I use tinned chopped tomatoes or fresh cherry tomatoes, and the creamy burrata on top of the pasta sauce gives a milky mouthful that is quite amazing.

400g/14oz egg *taglierini*
(page 74)

75ml/5 tablespoons olive oil, plus
extra for drizzling
5 garlic cloves, thinly sliced
1 x 400g/14oz tin chopped tomatoes
or 500g/1lb 2oz fresh datterini or
cherry tomatoes
handful of basil leaves
2 balls of burrata, halved
Parmesan, to serve

SERVES 4

In a medium saucepan, heat 45ml/3 tablespoons of the olive oil. Add the garlic and fry on a low heat until fragrant – about 1–2 minutes – then add the tomatoes and stir it all together.

Continue cooking for 20 minutes on the lowest heat, stirring from time to time and making sure the sauce doesn't stick to the bottom of the pan.

Crush the tomatoes gently with the back of a fork or a spoon, season to taste, then add the remaining olive oil and continue cooking for another 10–15 minutes.

Bring a large pan of water to the boil, add salt, then drop the *taglierini* into the water and cook for 1½–2 minutes.

Transfer the pasta to the tomato sauce, together with a ladleful of the pasta cooking water, and mix well by tossing or using a spatula. Check the seasoning – grind in some black pepper, maybe add a touch of salt – and finally drop in the basil and stir it all together one more time; if the sauce is too thick, add some more pasta water.

Divide between four plates and put half a ball of burrata on top of each one. Drizzle with olive oil and grate some Parmesan on top, because – why not!

VEGAN OPTION
Use *malloreddus* (page 106) instead of the egg *taglierini*.

Replace the cheeses with *pangrattato* (page 153).

ROASTED GARLIC TAGLIERINI

Garlic is the base of many good dishes; you just need to add lemon, herbs and seasoning and you've nailed the four tastes: sweet, sour, salt and heat. When I was growing up in Poland we ate lots of garlic – with greens, onions, potatoes, in soups and stews – but it wasn't until I came to England that I tried roasted garlic for the first time. I was blown away by its soft sweetness, and I love squeezing it out of its papery skin. If you haven't tried it before it's so simple and not an overpowering flavour at all.

400g/14oz egg *taglierini*
  (page 74)

2 large whole garlic bulbs
60ml/4 tablespoons olive oil
60g/2¼oz Parmesan, finely grated,
  plus extra to serve
bunch of parsley, chopped; I like
  to use curly parsley
4 tablespoons *pangrattato*
  (page 153), to serve (optional)

SERVES 4

Preheat the oven to 180°C fan/400°F/gas mark 6.

Cut 1cm/½in off the top of the garlic bulbs so the cloves are exposed (this makes it easier to squeeze it out later). Loosely wrap in kitchen foil and roast in the oven for 35–40 minutes until soft, then allow to cool.

Squeeze the garlic cloves into a medium saucepan, mash with the back of a spoon or fork, then add the olive oil with some ground black pepper. Cook on a low heat for 2 minutes until combined, then remove from the heat.

Bring a large pan of water to the boil before adding salt, then cook the *taglierini* for 1½ –2 minutes.

Return the sauce to the heat, adding a ladleful of the pasta cooking water. Transfer the pasta to the sauce using tongs and toss together, making sure the sauce coats the pasta, adding some more water if necessary.

Scatter the Parmesan all over the pasta and combine again. Then add the parsley and some sea salt and mix well. Check the seasoning and serve, scattering more Parmesan over each plate and ideally some *pangrattato* to give a lovely crunch.

TUNA TAGLIERINI WITH CHERRY TOMATOES

A tin of tuna is a great kitchen stand-by which, along with tinned tomatoes and a jar or two of olives, can always be found in my store cupboard at home. Here you can see how simplicity – working with what you have in your kitchen – gives such great flavour. You will need a couple of handfuls of cherry tomatoes and something green to freshen the sauce, then in 20 minutes, supper can be on the table.

400g/14oz egg *taglierini*
   (page 74)

60ml/4 tablespoons olive oil
3 garlic cloves, sliced
250g/9oz cherry tomatoes
1 x 200g/7oz tin tuna in oil (approx.
   150g/5½oz drained weight)
100g/3½oz wild garlic, spinach or
   handful of fresh parsley, chopped
juice of ½ lemon
pecorino, to serve

SERVES 4

Heat the olive oil in a large saucepan on a medium heat, then fry the garlic for 1 minute until slightly golden. Lower the heat, add the cherry tomatoes and cook for 10 minutes until they burst and soften.

Drain the oil from the tuna. If you like, you can add some of the oil to the sauce, but otherwise discard it. Using your fingers, break up the fish into small pieces and add to the pan with the tomatoes. Continue cooking on a low heat, stirring from time to time.

Bring a large pan of water to the boil, add salt, and cook the *taglierini* for 1½–2 minutes.

Just before lifting the cooked pasta out of the pan, add the greens to the sauce with half a ladleful of pasta cooking water so that the greens wilt a little. Then, using tongs, transfer the pasta to the sauce and mix together. Season with salt, freshly ground black pepper and the lemon juice, to taste.

Serve with shavings of pecorino and some fresh bread if you have any – it's always good to soak up the last of the sauce from your plate. So simple, so good.

CRAB WITH SQUID-INK TAGLIERINI

I had never eaten crab before I came to England, and now I dream of eating it in brown bread sandwiches at the seaside. White crab meat is not as strongly flavoured as brown and is just right for this dish, delicate and delicious combined with lemon, chilli and garlic. Buy it at a good fishmonger's or fish counter at the supermarket. The squid ink that colours the pasta will carry just a hint of the sea, so is a perfect match for crab.

400g/14oz squid-ink egg *taglierini* (page 74), or a mixture of squid ink and egg, as pictured

60ml/4 tablespoons olive oil
3 garlic cloves, finely chopped
2 mild, medium-sized red chillies, deseeded and finely chopped
150g/5½oz cherry tomatoes, halved
200g/7oz crab meat (ideally white, or a mix of brown and white)
juice of 1 lemon
handful of parsley, finely chopped
pangrattato (page 153), to serve

SERVES 4

Set a large saucepan over a low heat, warm the olive oil and add the garlic and chilli. Cook, stirring occasionally, until soft and fragrant, which will take about 5 minutes. Add the tomatoes and cook them down until they feel soft when you gently press them with the spoon. Keep on a low heat until the pasta is ready.

Bring a large pan of water to the boil before adding salt, and cook the *taglierini* for 1½–2 minutes, then lift it out of the pan with tongs and drop it into the sauce. The cooking water will cling to the pasta strands, which will help loosen the sauce.

Now add another ladleful of the pasta cooking water to the sauce, stir in the crab meat, the lemon juice and parsley, and toss everything together to coat the pasta with the sauce.

Divide between four bowls and serve with crunchy *pangrattato* and a fresh green salad on the side.

CHITARRA

Chitarra means 'guitar' in Italian, a reference to the strings stretched across the wooden frame of the *chitarra* pasta cutter. It reminds me a bit of an old-style egg-slicer. The cutter comes with a small rolling pin to push the pasta dough through the strings to make the shape known as *spaghetti alla chitarra*. It's really fun to make and one that kids may like to have a go at, too. You can easily find a *chitarra* online or you may be able to pick one up on your travels in Italy.

You can make *chitarra* using either egg or vegan dough.

Start with half the dough, keeping the other half tightly wrapped, and prepare a tray or baking sheet dusted with coarse semolina, ready to lay out your finished pasta.

Following the method on page 40, roll out your pasta dough, stopping at setting 7. If you prefer a bit more bite to the cooked pasta, stop at setting 6.

Cut the sheets into pieces that match the size of your *chitarra* box. Dust each sheet generously with semolina and stack them as you cut them.

Place one sheet on top of the strings. Dust with more semolina and then, using a rolling pin, roll back and forth across the strings so that the dough falls through them into the box below.

Take out the pasta strands and place them on the tray. Dust with more semolina and leave to one side until you're ready to cook.

CHITARRA ALLA GENOVESE

The classic pesto from Genoa is made with basil, garlic, pine nuts and olive oil, and everybody seems to love it. This dish is full of the beautiful flavours of spring and summer, so serve the pasta in a large bowl set in the middle of the table – preferably outside – and let everyone help themselves. The addition of new potatoes and crunchy beans makes this quite a filling dish. I leave out the garlic in my sauce to let the basil take centre stage. You can use *tagliatelle* instead of *chitarra* if you like.

400g/14oz egg *chitarra*
  (page 82)

250g/9oz new potatoes, scrubbed
200g/7oz green beans, ends trimmed
30g/¼ cup pine nuts
bunch of basil (approx. 30g/1oz)
juice of ½ lemon
¼ teaspoon salt
40g/1½oz Parmesan, grated, plus
  extra to serve
100–130ml/7–9 tablespoons olive oil

SERVES 4

Boil the new potatoes in salted water until cooked but still retaining a bite (this should take 12–15 minutes). Transfer to a separate dish and allow to cool before chopping them into small pieces.

Using the same cooking water, blanch the green beans – for no longer than 1½–2 minutes – then lift into a bowl of ice-cold water to cool. When the beans are chilled, remove from the water and slice into thumb-sized lengths.

Using a food processor or a mini chopper, blitz half the pine nuts for 10 seconds, then add the basil, lemon juice, salt, Parmesan and, to start with, a drizzle of olive oil. Start blitzing the ingredients, slowly adding the remaining olive oil as you go. When ready, transfer to a large saucepan and add the potatoes and beans.

Bring a large pan of water to the boil before adding salt, then cook the *chitarra* for 1½–2 minutes.

Warm the pesto on a low–medium heat with a ladleful of the pasta cooking water. Add the pasta to the pan, reserving some more water in case you need to loosen the sauce. Combine all the ingredients together, moving the pasta around the pan with kitchen tongs or a spatula. As always, check the seasoning.

Roughly chop the remaining pine nuts and finish the dish with more Parmesan and the chopped nuts. Such a feast!

VEGAN OPTION
Use vegan dough for the *chitarra* (page 31).

Use nutritional yeast instead of Parmesan.

CHITARRA WITH ANCHOVY, CHILLI, GARLIC & ROCKET

Anchovies bring a distinctive punch of flavour to any dish, and they're often used to give that umami depth to tomato sauces, salsas and tapenades. I buy jars of Mediterranean anchovies packed in olive oil and love the way they just melt into the dish when they're cooked – it's like magic. Combined with garlic, chillies and peppery rocket (arugula), this pasta packs plenty of flavour. Try serving it with a decent red – *perfetto!*

400g/14oz egg *chitarra*
(page 82)

60ml/4 tablespoons olive oil
4 garlic cloves, thinly sliced
2 medium red chillies, deseeded and
finely chopped
12 anchovy fillets
½ bunch of parsley, finely chopped
100g/3½oz rocket (arugula) or
spinach, washed
Parmesan or *pangrattato* (page 153),
or both, to serve

SERVES 4

Heat the olive oil in a large saucepan and fry the garlic for about 45 seconds until it's nice and fragrant, then add the red chilli. Continue to cook on a low heat for 5 minutes.

When the chilli and garlic are lovely and soft, add the anchovy fillets to the pan. As they cook, they will melt, creating a delicious sauce. At this point, add 50ml/3½ tablespoons of water and take the pan off the heat.

Bring a large pan of water to the boil before adding salt, then cook the *chitarra* for 1½–2 minutes.

Put the pan of sauce back on the heat and start to warm gently. When the pasta is cooked, use tongs to transfer it to the sauce, then add the parsley and rocket (arugula) and toss it all together. You may need to add some more cooking water to make sure all the pasta is coated with the anchovy sauce. Check the seasoning.

Divide between four plates and serve with Parmesan or *pangrattato* – I can never choose so I use both.

CHITARRA ALLA GRICIA

Guanciale is an Italian cured meat made from pigs' cheeks which, when cooked, is both melt-in-the-mouth and crispy depending on how long you cook it. The rich, fatty, salty taste means there's nothing better than finishing with *la scarpetta* – a piece of bread that you use to mop up the sauce from the plate, Italian-style. I like to use a smoky pecorino sardo in this dish, but if you can't get it then pecorino romano will give a beautiful soft finish instead.

400g/14oz egg *chitarra*
  (page 82)

1 tablespoon olive oil
200–250g/7–9oz *guanciale*, or
  pancetta with skin removed, cut
  into 1cm/½in strips
80g/3oz pecorino, grated, plus
  extra to serve

SERVES 4

Heat the olive oil in a large frying pan and add the *guanciale*. Cook on a medium heat until it's crispy and golden – around 12 minutes – but keep an eye on the heat to make sure the meat doesn't catch. If you prefer the *guanciale* to be softer, simply reduce the cooking time to around 7 minutes (but why would you not like the crispy bits?). When it's ready, grind some pepper over it and take the pan off the heat.

Meanwhile, bring a large pan of water to the boil before adding salt, then cook the *chitarra* for 1½–2 minutes.

When the pasta is cooked, transfer it to the sauce, add half a ladleful of pasta cooking water and return to the heat. Toss the pasta or turn it in with tongs, adding more water if necessary and making sure the *chitarra* is well coated in sauce. Turn off the heat, then gently scatter the cheese all over the pasta and mix together.

Serve with more pecorino cheese – there's never enough good cheese on pasta! – and some fresh bread like *focaccia* or sourdough to soak up every last drop of sauce.

LASAGNE

Who doesn't love the generous layers of pasta, rich sauce and toasty cheese topping of a deep-dish *lasagne* placed to share in the centre of the table? You can almost hear it singing an Italian *aria* when it emerges piping hot from the oven! It's a fantastic dish to bake when you have friends or family round, and you'll want to prepare it ahead – that way you don't miss out on the drinks and chat before dinner.

I suggest you make the sauces for your *lasagne* before rolling out your pasta dough, as once you've blanched the pasta you can then assemble the layers straight away. This is why I've included detailed instructions for pasta rolling in the recipes that follow. Do use the photos here as a guide though.

The white sauce, overleaf, is used in all the *lasagne* recipes and can be made a day ahead if you like – just cover and leave it in the fridge. White sauce also freezes really well, which is worth doing so you always have some to hand.

Don't be put off by all the different elements of *lasagne*; it's worth making for the smiles you get when you bring it to the table. You can also make ahead and leave it in the fridge for up to 48 hours or freeze it to eat later.

WHITE SAUCE FOR LASAGNE

I use oat milk instead of dairy because it brings a really delicious, nutty flavour that is so good with Parmesan, but of course you can use cow's milk if you prefer. To make it vegan, simply use 70g/2½oz nutritional yeast in place of the Parmesan, checking and adjusting the seasoning as you go.

50g/2oz olive oil or butter
50g/2oz plain or Italian 00 flour
750–850ml/1½–1¾ US pints oat milk
    or cow's milk
70g/2½oz Parmesan, grated
    (or nutritional yeast)
½ nutmeg, grated
zest of 1 lemon
1 teaspoon fine sea salt
½ teaspoon freshly ground black
    pepper

MAKES 900ML/2 US PINTS

Melt the olive oil or butter in a medium saucepan and add the flour. Combine together with a wooden spoon or a whisk to make a roux, and continue to cook on a low heat for 5 minutes, stirring occasionally.

Warm the milk in a small pan, but don't let it boil.

Start to pour the warm milk slowly into the roux, mixing with a whisk to create a nice smooth sauce. Hold back about 100ml/ 7 tablespoons of the milk – you're aiming for a sauce that has the consistency of double cream. If it's too thick, loosen with the remaining milk. Continue to cook on a low–medium heat, adding the Parmesan or nutritional yeast, nutmeg and lemon zest. Season with the salt and black pepper.

Check the seasoning one more time and you are ready to go.

AUTUMN LASAGNE WITH MUSHROOMS & CHESTNUTS

This is a good *lasagne* to serve in the cooler days of autumn (fall) when there are plenty of mushrooms about. Vibrant green sheets of spinach pasta and a creamy mushroom filling – a welcoming dish to share after a long walk. You can leave out the chestnuts if you're not a fan, but they do make this feel like a really special dish, perfect for a dinner party.

600g/1lb 5oz spinach egg *lasagne* (1½ x quantity of the recipe on page 32) for a 26 x 20cm/10 x 8in baking dish

45ml/3 tablespoons olive oil
3 garlic cloves, finely sliced
650g/1lb 7oz chestnut or mixed mushrooms, sliced
½ bunch of thyme, leaves picked
¼ teaspoon fine sea salt
900ml/2 US pints white sauce (opposite)
200g/7oz spinach, washed and chopped
180g/6oz cooked chestnuts, chopped (I use vacuum-packed)
1 ball of burrata or buffalo mozzarella, sliced
80g/3oz Parmesan, grated, plus extra to serve

SERVES 4-6

Heat the olive oil in a large frying pan and fry the garlic on a low heat for about 45 seconds until fragrant, then add the mushrooms and thyme and sauté for 10 minutes. The juices should be just beginning to run from the mushrooms. Add the fine sea salt, mix well and take off the heat.

Start making the white sauce (opposite) or retrieve it from the fridge if you made it earlier. Place in a medium saucepan and heat it through, then add the mushroom mixture, spinach, chestnuts and burrata or mozzarella. The sauce will be ready when the cheese has melted into it and everything is nicely combined.

Roll out the pasta following the method on page 40, stopping at setting 7. You will probably want to roll half the dough at a time, so keep the other half well wrapped until you're ready to use it. Cut the sheets to the rough size of your baking dish and lightly dust each one with semolina to avoid them sticking. You may need to double up the layers slightly to make them fit the dish, as the width of each sheet is governed by the size of your pasta machine, but a few overlaps or gaps are absolutely fine.

Bring a large pan of water to the boil before adding salt. Prepare a bowl of iced water and place it near the stove. Blanch each spinach pasta sheet for 30 seconds (do this one at a time), then immediately transfer to the iced water using tongs. Leave them in the iced water for a minute to thoroughly cool, then lay them out to dry on a clean tea (dish) towel. Don't use kitchen paper or you'll be picking off bits of paper later!

Preheat the oven to 170°C fan/375°F/gas mark 5.

CONTINUED...

To assemble the *lasagne*, spread a large spoonful of sauce all over the bottom of the dish. Next add a sheet or two of pasta, then a layer of white sauce, spreading it evenly to the edges of the dish, and lastly scatter over some Parmesan. Repeat each layer five more times, finishing with a layer of white sauce. Try to roughly divide the ingredients to allow for six layers, but if you haven't done it exactly, it will still taste delicious. After spreading the final layer of white sauce, cover the dish tightly with foil.

Bake for 30 minutes, then remove the foil and scatter over some more Parmesan. Return to the oven for another 15 minutes until the sauce is bubbling and the edges are nice and crispy.

Remove the *lasagne* from the oven and leave to rest for 10 minutes to firm up – it will be much easier to cut then. Serve with more Parmesan and a big bowl of greens on the side.

VEGAN OPTION

Use dried vegan *lasagne* sheets instead of fresh egg dough *lasagne*.

Use oat milk and olive oil to make the white sauce.

Replace the Parmesan and burrata with extra seasoning and top the dish with 4 tablespoons of *pangrattato* (page 153).

LASAGNE WITH SPICY SAUSAGE RAGÙ

Roasted hot red (bell) peppers give 'nduja a real spicy kick, which I love.
This is a rich ragù, which will melt into the layers of white sauce to create
a delicious, creamy, moreish pasta dish. What could be better than that?

600g/1lb 5oz egg *lasagne*
(1½ x quantity of the recipe on
page 26) for a 26 x 20cm/10 x 8in
baking dish

450ml/scant 2 cups white sauce
(page 90)
1 x quantity of sausage, fennel, 'nduja
ragù (page 109)
olive oil, for drizzling
80g/3oz Parmesan, grated

SERVES 4-6

Prepare the spicy 'nduja ragù (page 109) and keep it warm over
a low heat.

Now make the white sauce (page 90) or retrieve it from the
fridge and leave it to reach room temperature; there's no need
to heat it through as it will soon be bubbling in the oven.

Preheat the oven to 170°C fan/375°F/gas mark 5.

Roll out the pasta following the method on page 40, stopping at
setting 7. You will probably want to roll half the dough at a time,
so keep the other half well wrapped until you're ready to use it.
Cut the sheets to the rough size of your baking dish and lightly
dust each one with semolina to avoid them sticking.

Bring a large pan of water to the boil before adding salt.
Prepare a bowl of iced water and place it near the stove.
Blanch each pasta sheet for 30 seconds (do this one at a time),
then immediately transfer to the iced water using tongs. Leave
them in the iced water for a minute to thoroughly cool, then lay
them out to dry on a clean tea (dish) towel. Don't use kitchen
paper or you'll be picking off bits of paper later!

Spread a large spoonful of white sauce over the bottom of
the dish, then place your first sheet of pasta over the top (if
you need to, use two, depending on how large you've rolled
your sheets and bearing in mind you want to create six layers
altogether). Next add a layer of ragù, another spoonful of white
sauce, and lastly scatter over some Parmesan. Repeat until
you have six layers, finishing with a layer of white sauce, and
reserving a little Parmesan.

Cover the dish with foil and bake for 30 minutes. Remove from
the oven, take off the foil and scatter the top with remaining
Parmesan. Bake for another 15–20 minutes until the edges are
crispy and the sauce is piping hot.

Leave the *lasagne* to rest for 10 minutes to firm up – it will be
much easier to cut into slices. Serve with a fresh dressed salad
and a glass of good red wine. *Buon appetito!*

LASAGNE WITH SUMMER VEGETABLES

I love cartoons and animated films and, being a chef, of course I liked Pixar's *Ratatouille* ('You think cooking is a cute job, eh?'). In the summer we eat a lot of ratatouille, roasting all the vegetables in the oven and eating it with chunks of bread, French-style. Ratatouille makes a great base for *lasagne* because both recipes are all about layers of flavour. I've left out the peppers traditional to ratatouille here, but if you like you can add them, or good-quality olives and capers, to the tomato sauce – it'll be amazing!

600g/1lb 5oz egg *lasagne*
  (1½ x quantity of the recipe on
  page 26) for a 26 x 20cm/10 x 8in
  baking dish

FOR THE TOMATO SAUCE
60ml/4 tablespoons olive oil
4 garlic cloves, sliced
3 x 400g/14oz tins chopped tomatoes
1 teaspoon fine sea salt

FOR THE VEGETABLES
2 medium aubergines (eggplants),
  cut into 2.5cm/1in cubes
olive oil, for drizzling
2 medium courgettes (zucchini),
  sliced
½ bunch of basil, leaves only

900ml/2 US pints white sauce
  (page 90)
80g/3oz Parmesan, grated, plus
  extra to serve (optional)

SERVES 4–6

First, make the tomato sauce. Heat the olive oil in a large saucepan and fry the garlic for 45 seconds until fragrant, then add the tomatoes and cook on a low heat for 40–45 minutes. There's no need to put a lid on the pan, as you want the sauce to reduce down to intensify the flavour. At the end, season with the teaspoon of salt and leave to one side.

Meanwhile, place the aubergines (eggplants) in a large bowl, drizzle with olive oil and sprinkle with a couple of pinches of salt – mix well and set aside while you cook the courgettes (zucchini).

Heat a large frying pan, drizzle with olive oil and fry the courgettes (zucchini) on both sides until golden, then transfer to a separate bowl.

Add another couple of splashes of olive oil to the courgette (zucchini) pan and cook the aubergine (eggplant) until it's nice and soft, then transfer them to the bowl of courgettes (zucchini) and mix together. Fold in the basil leaves.

Next make the white sauce (page 90) or retrieve it from the fridge if you made it earlier. It should be at room temperature, but you don't need to reheat it – it will soon be bubbling hot in the oven.

Roll out the pasta following the method on page 40, stopping at setting 7. You will probably want to roll half the dough at a time, so keep the other half well wrapped. Cut the sheets to the rough size of your baking dish and lightly dust each one with semolina to avoid them sticking. You may need to double up the layers slightly to make them fit the dish, as the width of each sheet is governed by the size of your pasta machine, but a few overlaps or gaps are absolutely fine.

Bring a large pan of water to the boil before adding salt. Prepare a bowl of iced water and place it near the stove. Blanch each pasta sheet for 30 seconds (do this one at a time), then immediately transfer to the iced water using tongs. Leave the pasta in the iced water for a minute to cool thoroughly, then lay out each sheet to dry on a clean tea (dish) towel. Don't use kitchen paper or you'll be picking off bits of paper later!

Preheat the oven to 170°C fan/375°F/gas mark 5.

Now for the fun bit. To assemble the *lasagne*, spread a large spoonful of tomato sauce on the bottom of the baking dish, making sure it reaches into all the corners (this will stop the *lasagne* sticking to the bottom as it bakes). Next place a sheet or two of pasta on top, then spread another layer of tomato sauce, followed by a spoonful of the courgette (zucchini) and aubergine (eggplant) mix, then a layer of white sauce sprinkled with a handful of Parmesan. Make sure you spread every layer right up to the edges of the dish as far as you can, then repeat each layer five more times – pasta, tomato sauce, vegetables, white sauce, Parmesan – finishing with the last of the tomato sauce and white sauce only.

Cover with foil and bake for 30 minutes, then remove the foil, sprinkle the top with Parmesan, and bake for another 15 minutes until the sauce is bubbling and the edges are nice and crispy. Remove the *lasagne* from the oven and leave to rest for 10 minutes to rest and firm up – it will be much easier to cut.

Serve with more Parmesan and drizzle with olive oil if you fancy it (I always do!).

VEGAN OPTION

Use dried vegan *lasagne* sheets instead of fresh egg dough *lasagne*.

Use oat milk and olive oil to make the white sauce.

In the layers, replace the Parmesan with extra seasoning and top the dish with 4 tablespoons of *pangrattato* (page 153).

GARGANELLI

Garganelli is a tube shape, similar to penne. It is usually made on a garganelli board, which gives it ridges and more surface area to carry the pasta sauce. To avoid drying out, start with just a quarter portion of the dough, leaving the rest wrapped in clingfilm (plastic wrap) until you're ready to use it.

You will need a garganelli board and small rolling pin (this comes with the board). You shouldn't need to flour the board because the pasta will be starting to dry out anyway, but if the dough is sticking you can dust the board with a little coarse semolina.

Prepare a tray or baking sheet dusted with coarse semolina, ready to lay out your finished pasta.

Following the method on page 40, roll out your pasta dough, stopping at setting 7.

Cut the sheet into equal squares of about 4cm/1½in. Stack the squares on top of one another to avoid them drying out.

Place one square on the garganelli board at a 45-degree angle to the ridges, so the corners point towards the edges of the board.

Place the rolling pin across the middle of the dough then gently lift the bottom corner and wrap it over the pin, overlapping the top corner of dough. Tuck the bottom corner under the pin, and press gently to secure.

Roll the pin forwards to form a tube, pressing so that the board forms ridges on the pasta. The pressure of rolling sticks the corners neatly together to form a sturdy tube.

Slide the tube of pasta from the pin and place on the semolina-dusted tray. Repeat with the rest of the dough.

Note: you can also pinch together opposite sides of each square/rectangle into a pleat to create *farfalle*, meaning 'butterfly' pasta.

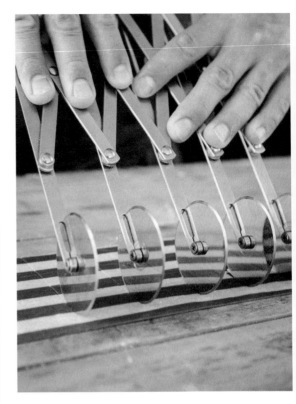

LAMB SHOULDER RAGÙ GARGANELLI

On the morning of the February *Sartiglia* in Sardinia, my friend Luca and I went to a house in the countryside where they had recently slaughtered a lamb. We were fascinated to watch the animal being butchered, and later that evening we shared a plate of lamb ragù with pasta. This dish always reminds me of the exciting, carnival atmosphere of that day. I prefer to pull the lamb once it is cooked and then add it to the ragù, while the spoonful of butter, although not at all traditional, adds a touch of creaminess to the sauce. This recipe makes more ragù than you'll need for four people – freeze the rest for use next time. *Bellissima!*

400g/14oz egg *garganelli*
(page 98)

½ lamb shoulder, on the bone
(around 1kg/2lb 4oz)
30ml/2 tablespoons olive oil
1 large onion, finely diced
1 large carrot, finely diced
½ head of celery, finely diced
4 garlic cloves, finely diced
large sprig of thyme
large sprig of rosemary
3 bay leaves
350ml/1½ cups white wine
1 x 400g/14oz tin plum tomatoes
drizzle of olive oil or 1 tablespoon
butter, if you prefer a creamy
texture
Parmesan, to finish

SERVES 4

Preheat the oven to 150°C fan/325°F/gas mark 3.

Season the lamb shoulder with salt and black pepper. In a frying pan on a medium heat, brown off the lamb on all sides until it's nice and bronzed. Transfer it to a casserole dish or heavy-bottomed oven tin that can be used on the hob and set aside.

In another pan, make the soffritto. Heat the olive oil on a low heat and gently sweat the onion, carrot and celery for 20 minutes, then add the garlic and fry for a further 2 minutes.

Add the soffritto to the lamb casserole dish, together with the herbs, wine and tomatoes, and set over a medium heat until it reaches a steady simmer.

Put the lid on the casserole dish and place in the oven for 4 hours or until the meat is very tender. It's a good idea to check halfway through and top up with water if the dish is looking a little dry.

When the lamb is cooked – it will be very tender and falling away from the bone – take it out of the oven. Pick out and discard the herb stems and bay leaves. Carefully lift the lamb onto a board or a large plate and set everything aside to cool.

Pour the liquid and vegetables into a bowl, checking to make sure there are no stray bones, then blitz using a hand blender or food processor. Pour the sauce into the cleaned casserole dish.

CONTINUED…

Once the lamb is cool enough to handle, pull all the meat from the bone, breaking apart any large pieces. Discard the bones and the fat and add the meat to the sauce. Place on a low heat, stir well to combine, then leave to simmer gently for 20 minutes. Check for seasoning. At this point, I transfer 320g/11½oz of the ragù to a separate saucepan and set aside the rest for freezing.

Bring a pan of water to the boil before adding the salt, then drop in the *garganelli* and cook for 1½–2 minutes.

Transfer the *garganelli* together with a ladleful of pasta cooking water to the sauce and add the olive oil or butter, combining everything together. Serve in a large bowl for sharing, with a chunk of Parmesan and a glass or two of good red wine.

GARGANELLI ALLA NORMA

Why is this recipe called Norma? Good question – you'll have to ask a Sicilian because everyone knows this dish there. I think it's to do with the perfection of an opera called *Norma*, and one day I might track it down and listen to it. The key ingredients are aubergine (eggplant), tomato and semi-hard, aged *ricotta salata*. I peel the aubergines (eggplants) because I prefer the softer texture when they're cooked without the skin – use a vegetable peeler to do this. If you can't find *ricotta salata* (you may track it down in a good deli or cheesemonger), then replace it with pecorino.

400g/14oz egg *garganelli*
(page 98)

2 medium aubergines (eggplants)
(approx. 500g/1lb 2oz), peeled
and cut into 2cm/¾in cubes
60ml/4 tablespoons olive oil, plus
extra for roasting
4 garlic cloves, thinly sliced
1 large onion, diced
1 x 400g/14oz tin cherry tomatoes,
chopped
½ teaspoon fine salt
handful of basil leaves
75g/3oz *ricotta salata* or pecorino

SERVES 4

Preheat the oven to 180°C fan/400°F/gas mark 6 and line a roasting tin with baking parchment.

Place the aubergine (eggplant) cubes on the tin, drizzle generously with olive oil, sprinkle with salt and mix together with your hands to ensure they are well coated with oil. Roast for 25–30 minutes until soft, shaking the tin halfway through the cooking time to ensure an even colour.

In a large saucepan, heat the olive oil on a medium heat and fry the garlic for 1 minute, then add the onion and cook for about 10 minutes until golden. Add the tomatoes and simmer for a further 10 minutes. When the aubergines (eggplants) are cooked, transfer them with all their juices into the sauce, add the fine salt, and cook on a low heat for 10–15 minutes until the sauce has thickened.

Bring a large pan of water to the boil before adding salt, then cook the *garganelli* for 1½–2 minutes.

Drain the pasta, setting aside a jugful of the cooking water. Loosen the sauce with a ladleful of the pasta water before adding the pasta. Combine everything together using a spatula, adding a little more water if you think it's needed. Fold in the basil and check the seasoning.

Serve with grated *ricotta salata* or pecorino on top. *Mamma mia!* – how I do love this dish!

VEGAN OPTION

Use *capunti* (page 116) instead of egg *garganelli*.

Finish with *pangrattato* (page 153) instead of cheese.

GARGANELLI WITH MISO, AUBERGINE & HERBS

I really like eating Japanese food and have always been curious about their cooking culture. I particularly love miso, so here I have combined its salty umami flavour with the soft sweetness of roasted aubergine (eggplant) and basil. Instead of using olive oil, I mix butter with the miso because it's easier to combine and less likely to split, and it creates a lovely glossy sauce. Red miso gives a more intense flavour, but you can use red or white, either will work.

400g/14oz egg *garganelli* (page 98)

2 aubergines (eggplants) (approx. 600g/1lb 5oz), peeled and chopped into small cubes
30ml/2 tablespoons olive oil
¼ teaspoon fine salt
4 teaspoons red miso
4 tablespoons butter, softened
bunch of parsley, leaves only, finely chopped
½ bunch of basil, leaves picked
50g/2oz Parmesan, grated

SERVES 4

Preheat the oven to 175°C fan/375°F/gas mark 5.

Combine the chopped aubergines (eggplants), olive oil and fine salt in a large bowl and mix well – I like using my hands to mix so I can feel that everything is well coated in the oil.

Line a roasting tin (sheet pan) with baking parchment and transfer the aubergines to the tin. Roast for 20–30 minutes until soft, then remove from the oven and allow to cool.

Using a spatula, combine the red miso and butter together in a small bowl until you have a lovely paste with an even colour.

Bring a large pan of water to the boil before adding salt, then cook the *garganelli* for 1½–2 minutes.

In the meantime, put a large saucepan on a medium heat, transfer half a ladleful of pasta cooking water to the pan and add the buttery miso paste, mixing well with a spatula to combine.

Transfer both the cooked pasta and the aubergines (eggplants) to the sauce, fold them together, then add the parsley and basil. Gently combine, then reduce the heat to low, scatter over the Parmesan and allow it to melt into the sauce. Divide between four plates and serve immediately.

GARGANELLI WITH CARAMELISED SHALLOTS & ANCHOVIES

I'm waiting to harvest my first ever crop of banana shallots, and there are so many that I'm going to learn how to plait them so they can be stored in the garden shed. I'll also be using some of them to make this dish. Caramelising the shallots brings out their soft sweetness, while the parsley gives a burst of freshness. And, of course, Parmesan to finish – Italians may say 'no cheese with fish', but try it here and you'll see it works really well.

400g/14oz egg *garganelli*
  (page 98)

60ml/4 tablespoons olive oil
5 garlic cloves, finely chopped
4 large banana (echalion) shallots
  (approx. 450g/1lb), sliced
  lengthways
½ teaspoon fine sea salt
2 teaspoons tomato purée
8–10 anchovy fillets
bunch of parsley, chopped
Parmesan or *pangrattato* (page 153),
  or both, to serve

SERVES 4

Heat the olive oil in a large saucepan and fry the garlic on a medium heat for a minute or so until fragrant. Add the shallots and cook for 10 minutes, then add the fine sea salt, cover the pan with a lid and continue cooking for another 10 minutes, stirring occasionally, until the shallots are nice and soft.

Stir in the tomato purée and anchovy fillets, lower the heat and cook for another 5 minutes until the anchovies have melted into the sauce. Grind over some black pepper and pour in 100ml/ 7 tablespoons of water. Leave on a low heat while you cook the pasta.

Bring a large pan of water to the boil before adding salt, then cook the *garganelli* for 1½–2 minutes.

Using a slotted spoon, transfer the pasta to the sauce. Combine them well and check the seasoning – the sauce may need a pinch of salt, another twist of pepper, or it may need to be loosened with some pasta cooking water. Finally, mix in the parsley and serve with the Parmesan and/or *pangrattato* scattered on top.

MALLOREDDUS

▼▼▼▼▼▼▼▼▼▼▼▼▼▼▼▼▼▼▼▼

This shape originated in Sardinia and is also known as *gnocchetti Sardi*. These are little rolls of pasta with a firm bite, quite different from silky egg pastas.

You don't need to rest this dough in the fridge before shaping; you can use it straight away. You can also dry it out if you like: just spread the shapes on a board dusted with coarse semolina and leave it uncovered for an hour or so. You can then store it in an airtight container and use it within two days.

Prepare a tray or baking sheet dusted with coarse semolina, ready to lay out your finished pasta.

Take one quarter of vegan semolina dough (page 31), keeping the rest well wrapped, and roll it into a long rope that is about the thickness of a pencil. Rolling it out like this is a bit like playing with plasticine – I love it!

Cut the pasta into pieces about 2.5–3cm/ 1–1¼in in length.

Take a *garganelli* board (page 98) and place a piece of dough onto the board. You will be rolling the dough along the lines of the board.

Using your thumb, a dough scraper or an ordinary table knife (it's worth trying all of them to see which works best for you; I use a dough scraper because it gives the neatest results), press down lightly on the dough so that it wraps around the blade of the scraper slightly, then push the scraper away from you across the board in one smooth motion so that the pasta forms a little roll, a bit like a butter curl. It does take some practice, but it is very satisfying once you get the hang of it.

Place the shapes on the tray while you roll out the rest of the dough.

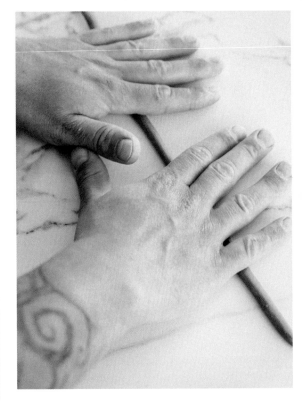

MALLOREDDUS WITH SAUSAGE, 'NDUJA & FENNEL RAGÙ

This ragù is full of beautiful aromatic flavours. Choose a really good-quality pork sausage, preferably from the butcher's, while you can find 'nduja at an Italian deli. I love the spicy kick of the 'nduja, but if you're not keen on the heat, then simply leave it out. You will have more sauce than you need for this dish, but you can easily freeze what you don't use (when you want to defrost it, just leave it overnight in the fridge).

400g/14oz vegan semolina *malloreddus* (page 106)

30ml/2 tablespoons olive oil
1 large onion, finely diced
1 small fennel bulb, finely diced
½ head of celery, finely diced
4 garlic cloves, finely diced
500g/1lb 2oz good-quality pork sausage
3 teaspoons fennel seeds, toasted and ground
½ teaspoon coriander seeds, toasted and ground
3 bay leaves
200ml/generous ¾ cup white wine
200ml/generous ¾ cup chicken stock (broth)
100g/3½oz 'nduja
3 tablespoons mascarpone
½ bunch of sage leaves, chopped
Parmesan, grated, to serve

SERVES 4

In a large saucepan, heat the olive oil and gently sweat the onion, fennel and celery for 20 minutes until soft and sweet, then add the garlic and fry for a further 2 minutes.

Squeeze the sausage meat out of the skins. In a separate pan, fry off the sausage meat on a high heat for 2–3 minutes, turning it to brown all over. You don't want to cook it all the way through, but do try to get a nice bit of colour.

Transfer the sausage meat to the pan with the vegetables, then add the ground seeds and bay leaves, the white wine and chicken stock (broth) and simmer gently for 1 hour (there's no need to put a lid on the pan).

Skim off any excess fat from the pan, then add the 'nduja and let it melt into the sauce. Check the seasoning and add salt and freshly ground black pepper, if needed. At this point, I measure out about 300g/10½oz into a separate pan and freeze the rest for the next time I make *malloreddus*.

Bring a large pan of water to the boil before adding salt, and cook the *malloreddus* for 3–4 minutes.

Meanwhile, add the mascarpone to the ragù and stir it in. When the pasta is cooked, transfer it to the sauce together with half a ladleful of pasta cooking water, scatter over the sage and stir everything together. Check the seasoning again, then serve straight away, with grated Parmesan on top.

MALLOREDDUS WITH ROASTED RED PEPPER

I used to work at a Spanish tapas restaurant in Bermondsey, and every day we roasted several trays of red (bell) peppers until the skins bubbled and blackened. We used them to make spicy Romesco sauce with almonds, garlic, chilli and red wine vinegar. This is a nod to that recipe, but here the sweetness of the roasted (bell) peppers is cut through with sharp lemon and pungent fresh basil. I still include the garlic and chilli, but I use walnuts instead of almonds. If you use *pangrattato* instead of Parmesan, you have a beautiful vegan dish.

400g/14oz vegan semolina
  malloreddus (page 106)

2 garlic cloves, in their skins
1 medium red chilli, stalk
  removed and deseeded
4 red (bell) peppers (approx.
  600g/1lb 5oz), tops removed
  and deseeded
60g/2¼oz walnuts
50g/2oz Parmesan, grated,
  plus extra to serve
45ml/3 tablespoons olive oil,
  plus extra for roasting
juice of ½ lemon
handful of basil

SERVES 4

Preheat the oven to 175°C fan/375°F/gas mark 5 and line a baking sheet with baking parchment.

Place the garlic, chilli and (bell) peppers on the baking sheet, drizzle with olive oil and roast for 30 minutes until soft and slightly blackened.

Meanwhile, on a separate baking sheet, roast the walnuts for 5 minutes. Allow all the ingredients to cool.

In a food processor, pulse the walnuts a couple of times, then squeeze the roasted garlic cloves out of their skins and into the processor along with the chilli and roasted (bell) peppers, the Parmesan, olive oil, lemon juice and some salt. Blend until you have a paste the texture of pesto. Transfer to a large saucepan and heat really slowly.

Bring a pan of water to the boil before adding salt, and cook the *malloreddus* for 3–4 minutes.

Transfer the pasta to the sauce and add half a ladleful of the cooking water, if needed, to loosen the sauce. Toss it all together and scatter over the basil leaves. Grind in some black pepper and add a pinch of salt if you think it needs it. Serve with Parmesan and some garlicky buttered spinach or broccoli on the side.

VEGAN OPTION
Finish with *pangrattato* (page 153) instead of Parmesan.

MALLOREDDUS WITH BROCCOLI, CHILLI & GARLIC

This dish is my love letter to broccoli, which I eat three or four times a week. It only takes 15 minutes to make and it's such an affordable, everyday pasta recipe. The broccoli is given a real lift with the chilli and garlic, while the lemon juice helps to keep the fresh green colour and flavour. I like using mild chillies, as spicy ones will overwhelm the dish, so check out the heat of your chillies by cutting off a tip and dabbing it on your tongue. You'll soon find out how hot they are!

400g/14oz vegan semolina
  malloreddus (page 106)

1 large head of broccoli or
  2 smaller ones
60ml/4 tablespoons olive oil
4 garlic cloves, finely chopped
2 medium red chillies, deseeded
  and finely chopped
30ml/2 tablespoons lemon juice
60g/2¼oz Parmesan, grated, plus
  extra to serve (optional)
pangrattato (page 153), to serve
  (optional)

SERVES 4

Bring a large pan of salted water to the boil on a high heat. Blanch the whole broccoli for 3–4 minutes, then use tongs to remove it from the boiling water – it should still be crunchy. Set aside until it's cool enough to handle, and keep the broccoli water to one side as well, as you can use it to cook the pasta.

Heat 30ml/2 tablespoons of the olive oil in a large saucepan, add the garlic and cook for 45 seconds until it's nice and fragrant, then add the chillies and continue to cook on a low heat for 3–4 minutes. When the chillies are just cooked through, take the pan off the heat.

Cut the stalk off the broccoli and chop it into small pieces. Put the pieces into a food processor or blender with 50ml/3½ tablespoons of the cooking water and the remaining olive oil and blend together until creamy. You may need to add more water.

Cut the broccoli florets into small pieces. Add them to the pan with the chilli and garlic, together with the blended broccoli stalk, and return the pan to a low heat to keep warm.

Meanwhile, bring your pan of broccoli water to the boil again, drop in the *malloreddus* and cook for 3–4 minutes until *al dente*, then lift out and add to the sauce, reserving a jugful of pasta water.

Combine the cooked pasta with the sauce and add some pasta water to loosen it if necessary. Add the lemon juice and scatter over the Parmesan, then toss it all together. Check the seasoning, adding salt and freshly ground black pepper if needed, then serve with more Parmesan or *pangrattato*, or both.

VEGAN OPTION
Use nutritional yeast instead of Parmesan.

MALLOREDDUS ALLA VODKA

This is the perfect pasta for a weekend supper with friends. It's quite rich, so I like to serve it with a mixed green salad and slices of *focaccia* or *ciabatta* to mop up the sauce. Once the onions have been softened, stir in the tomato paste; it will catch on the bottom of the pan, so adding the vodka on a low heat will dissolve all that intense tomato flavour back into the sauce.

400g/14oz vegan semolina
malloreddus (page 106)

30ml/2 tablespoons olive oil
3 medium shallots, thinly sliced
3 garlic cloves, finely chopped
¼ teaspoon chilli flakes
40g/1½oz tomato paste
75ml/5 tablespoons vodka
150g/5½oz mascarpone
30g/1oz butter (optional)
70g/2½oz Parmesan, grated

SERVES 4

In a large saucepan, heat the olive oil and add the shallots, garlic and chilli flakes. Cook on a medium heat for 5–8 minutes until the shallots are soft and golden but not browned, stirring occasionally. Add the tomato paste and keep cooking for 5 minutes on a low–medium heat, so that the tomato paste coats the shallots and garlic and absorbs their flavours.

Move the pan to the smallest ring on the hob and set it on a really low heat to avoid lighting the alcohol as you add it. Once you have added the vodka, leave it to bubble for a few minutes to allow the alcohol to evaporate, then add 50ml/3½ tablespoons of water and the mascarpone. Stir until the cheese has completely melted into the sauce, then take it off the heat.

Bring a large pan of water to the boil before adding salt, then drop in the *malloreddus*. Cook for 3–4 minutes, then drain the pasta, reserving a small jugful of cooking water in case you need to loosen the sauce.

Put the sauce back on a medium–low heat, transfer the pasta into the pan and combine it all together. Stir in the butter, if using – this will give you a really lovely glossy texture. Scatter Parmesan all over the pasta and mix it in. Taste it – you may need to add a touch of salt and a grind of black pepper, or to loosen the sauce with some of the reserved pasta cooking water. Serve in a large bowl and you are ready to go!

VEGAN OPTION
Use almond cream or almond milk instead of the mascarpone.

Use nutritional yeast instead of Parmesan for the salty, umami taste.

MALLOREDDUS WITH MINT CACIO E PEPE

My friends Khyati and Nokx formed a Wednesday evening running club called Pasta & Pie (Nokx works at the Holborn Dining Rooms, which is famous for its intricate pies). To be honest, we sometimes eat more than we run, but *c'est la vie*. One day we made *cacio e pepe* sauce together and somehow a handful of mint went into the dish too – we loved the fresh, minty flavour with the splashes of green leaf in the sauce.

The knack to making this dish is to avoid overheating the sauce when you add the Parmesan to the pasta, pepper and butter, otherwise the cheese will go stringy. It's also easier to create a nice glossy sauce if you scatter the cheese when you add it rather than dropping it in as a heap. *Cacio e pepe* is not traditionally made with butter – just cheese and water – but I like creamy sauces and if the dish is tasty, well, I'm happy to break with tradition.

400g/14oz vegan semolina *malloreddus* (page 106)

75g/2¾oz butter
4 teaspoons coarsely ground black pepper
80g/3oz Parmesan (a 50/50 mix of pecorino and Parmesan would be perfect, but just Parmesan is great too), grated
juice of ½ lemon
½ bunch of mint, chopped (approx. 10g/⅓oz)

SERVES 4

Bring a large pan of water to the boil before adding salt, drop in the *malloreddus* and cook for 3–4 minutes.

At the same time, take a ladleful of the pasta cooking water from the boiling pot, add it to another pan with the butter on a low heat and stir until the butter has melted – you want to create an emulsion that will perfectly coat the pasta. When you have achieved this, add the pepper and the cooked pasta, making sure to reserve a jugful of the pasta cooking water.

Now – and this is really important – scatter the cheese around the pan and don't let it come to the boil. Squeeze in the lemon juice and sprinkle with mint. Toss or mix well until the sauce is glossy, adding a little more water if needed – the consistency should be similar to double cream.

Check the seasoning as it may well need a pinch or two of salt. I like serving this with steamed garlicky greens on the side.

CAPUNTI

▼▼▼▼▼▼▼▼▼▼▼▼▼▼▼▼▼▼▼▼

I really like how much this shape has the look of an empty pea pod; the little dips formed by your fingertips are just made to carry the sauce. You can roll *capunti* on a *garganelli* board (page 98) or simply use a clean kitchen worktop.

You don't need to rest this dough in the fridge before shaping; you can use it straight away. You can also dry it out if you like: just spread the shapes on a board dusted with coarse semolina and leave it uncovered for an hour or so. You can then store it in an airtight container and use it within two days.

Prepare a tray or baking sheet dusted with coarse semolina, ready to lay out your finished pasta.

Take one quarter of vegan semolina dough (page 31), keeping the rest well wrapped, and roll it into a long rope that is about the thickness of a pencil.

Cut the roll into pieces about 4cm/1½in long.

Take a piece of dough, place it on the *garganelli* board or worktop and, using two or three fingers, press it and slide it towards you at the same time. The first few times you try this you may squash the dough by pressing a bit too hard, which means it won't roll, but you'll soon get the hang of it after a few attempts.

Place the shapes on the tray while you roll out the rest of the dough.

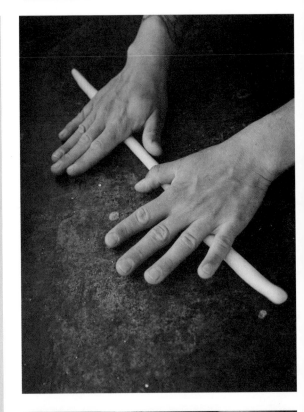

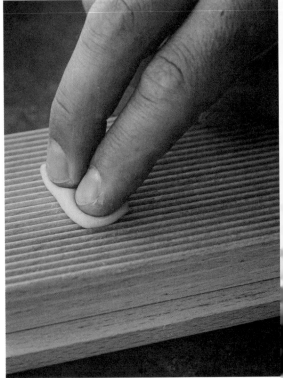

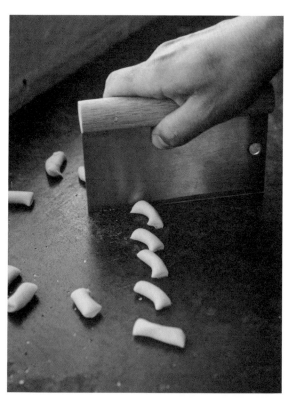

CAPUNTI WITH WILD GARLIC PESTO & ALMONDS

This sauce reminds me of going for spring walks in the local woodland with my partner, Elizabeth. It's such a beautiful time of year, when everything is so fresh and green, and it's really nice to come home with a bag of wild garlic leaves. Sometimes we gather so much that I make a large batch of pesto and freeze it in small containers – it keeps really well in the freezer for 6 to 8 months and you will be able to conjure up a summery dish to cheer a winter supper. If you can't find wild garlic, you can use basil, mint or rocket (arugula) instead.

400g/14oz vegan spinach *capunti* (page 116)

30g/⅓ cup almonds
2 large handfuls of wild garlic, washed
juice of ½ lemon
100ml/7 tablespoons olive oil
½ teaspoon salt
60g/2¼oz Parmesan, grated, plus extra to serve
pangrattato, to serve

SERVES 4

First, roast the almonds. Preheat the oven to 170°C fan/375°F/gas mark 5. Spread the almonds on a small baking sheet and roast for 5–7 minutes, then allow them to cool before tipping into a food processor. Pulse the almonds until you get small, coarse pieces.

Add the wild garlic and lemon juice to the processor and start blending, slowly pouring in the olive oil as you go, and adding the salt and Parmesan at the end. Transfer the pesto to a large saucepan.

Bring another large pan filled with water to the boil before adding salt, and cook the *capunti* for 3–4 minutes.

Heat the pan of pesto, adding a ladleful of the pasta cooking water. Drain the pasta, keeping aside a jugful of cooking water in case you need more, and transfer the pasta to the sauce. Continue cooking on a low heat, tossing the pasta until it is combined with the pesto, adding some extra cooking water if needed. Serve with more Parmesan grated over and some *pangrattato* generously sprinkled on top.

VEGAN OPTION
Use 4 tablespoons *pangrattato* (page 153) or 3 tablespoons nutritional yeast, plus extra to serve, instead of the Parmesan.

CAPUNTI WITH SARDINES, FENNEL, HERBS & LEMON

Sardines are really healthy fish to eat, full of calcium, omega-3 oils and vitamin B12. OK, they do have a strong flavour and the tiny bones are fiddly, but it's worth persisting as this is a fresh, herby dish that I hope you will be tempted to try. Serve this in a large bowl set in the middle of the table, scatter with *pangrattato* and eat with a green salad or garlicky broccoli.

400g/14oz vegan semolina *capunti*
   (page 116)

30ml/2 tablespoons olive oil
2 banana shallots, thinly sliced
3 garlic cloves, chopped
2 small fennel bulbs, diced as
   small as you can
2 bay leaves
1 teaspoon ground fennel seeds
1 x 140g/5½oz tin of sardines in
   olive oil
zest and juice of 1 lemon
bunch of dill, chopped
bunch of parsley, chopped
pangrattato (page 153), to serve

SERVES 4

In a large saucepan, heat the olive oil on a medium heat, then add the shallots, garlic, fennel and bay leaves and cook for 10–15 minutes until soft, stirring every few minutes. Add the ground fennel seeds and cook for another 2 minutes until the sauce is golden brown and fragrant.

Use your fingers to halve each sardine, remove the bones and break the sardines into chunks, discarding the oil. Add the sardines and lemon zest to the sauce and cook for a further minute, then take off the heat.

Bring a large pan of water to the boil before adding salt, and cook the *capunti* for 3–4 minutes.

Scoop out a ladleful of the pasta cooking water and add it to the sauce. Return the saucepan to the heat. Drain the pasta, keeping a jugful of cooking water in case you need more, and transfer the pasta to the sauce. Combine them together, then season with salt flakes and freshly ground black pepper.

Add the lemon juice and the chopped herbs, and toss a few times so the sauce coats the pasta nicely, before transferring to a large serving bowl. Serve with a bowl of *pangratto* to scatter on top.

RAVIOLI

If you want to create the frilled edges of classic *ravioli*, you will need a *ravioli* cutter. I also keep a glass of chilled water and a pastry brush to hand when I'm making this shape, as the dough sometimes dries out as it's worked.

You can freeze *ravioli*: put the whole tray in the freezer so that they freeze as individual pieces; once frozen, you can store them together.

Prepare a tray or baking sheet dusted with coarse semolina, ready to lay out your finished pasta.

Take about a quarter of your dough, keeping the rest well wrapped. Following the method on page 40, roll out your dough, stopping at setting 8.

Fold a sheet in half lengthways and press down lightly on the fold to mark the centre. Spread the sheet out flat again.

Drop teaspoons of filling just above the fold line with a thumb-width space between each spoonful, along the length of the dough.

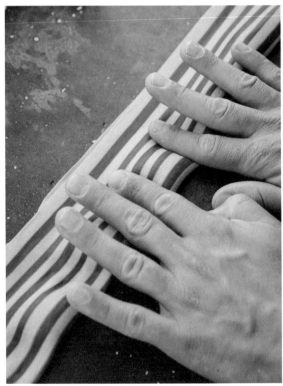

Using a pastry brush or your finger, dab a little water carefully around each spoonful of filling, then fold the dough over so that the long edges meet. Press together to seal. Press down quite hard between the little mounds of filling. Look out for any air pockets that may have formed and push the air away and out of the edges – this will prevent the *ravioli* from splitting when you cook them.

This part is fun. Using a *ravioli* cutter or a sharp knife, cut along the length of the dough and in between each mound to create individual pieces of *ravioli*.

Lift each one onto the dusted tray, then dust again with a little more coarse semolina while you roll and fill the next batch of dough.

PUMPKIN & WALNUT RAVIOLI

This makes a really fun supper for friends, and as I always think of both the purple beetroot (beet) and orange pumpkin as earthy, hearty ingredients, perfect for autumn (fall); why not serve it as a Hallowe'en or Thanksgiving dish?

200g/7oz beetroot egg dough
   (page 34)
200g/7oz classic or rich egg dough
   (pages 26 & 27)

500g/1lb 2oz pumpkin or squash,
   deseeded and cut in half
2 sprigs of rosemary, leaves finely
   chopped
½ teaspoon salt
70g/2½oz Parmesan, grated,
   plus extra to serve
½ nutmeg
75g/2¾oz butter
100g/3½oz walnuts, chopped,
   to serve

SERVES 4

Preheat the oven to 175°C fan/375°F/gas mark 5, and line a baking sheet with baking parchment. Put the pumpkin or squash halves on the baking sheet and roast for 30–40 minutes until soft (you don't need to drizzle with olive oil, but you can if you like). When it's ready, take it out of the oven and allow to cool.

Scrape the pumpkin flesh from the skin using a metal spoon and place it in a food processor with the rosemary, salt and Parmesan. Pulse to create a smooth paste. If you don't have a food processor, use a ricer or potato masher and finish with a spatula to smooth out any lumps.

Transfer the mixture to a clean bowl and grate over the nutmeg, then mix well and taste to check the seasoning. Cover the bowl with clingfilm (plastic wrap) and leave the filling in the fridge for 30 minutes to set.

Meanwhile, make your stripy dough (page 44), then roll and fill your *ravioli* (page 122) with the chilled pumpkin mixture and set on a semolina-dusted tray.

Next, make the brown butter. Place a small saucepan on a medium heat and add the butter. Swirl the pan from time to time to make sure the butter is cooking evenly, and cook until the butter browns and you smell its lovely, nutty flavour. Take off the heat and strain into a large saucepan (this is to avoid any dark brown bits spoiling the texture of the sauce).

Bring a large pan of salted water to the boil and cook the *ravioli*, a few at a time, for 1½–2 minutes.

Put the pan of brown butter back on the heat, adding half a ladleful of pasta cooking water, then transfer the *ravioli* into the sauce using a slotted spoon. Move the *ravioli* really gently around the pan to make sure they are all well covered with sauce. Scatter over the chopped walnuts and some more Parmesan, and serve.

TRIANGOLI

▼▼▼▼▼▼▼▼▼▼▼▼▼▼▼▼▼▼▼▼▼

This filled pasta is just like *ravioli*, but triangular in shape. What more can I say?

Prepare a tray or baking sheet dusted with coarse semolina, ready to lay out your finished pasta.

Start with about a quarter of the dough, keeping the rest of it well wrapped. I like to keep a glass of chilled water and a pastry brush to hand, too, as the dough can sometimes dry out as it's worked. A dab of water helps to seal the edges.

Following the method on page 40, roll out your pasta dough, stopping at setting 8.

Cut out evenly sized squares, about 6–7cm/2½–2¾in square.

Pipe or place a teaspoon of filling in the middle of each square.

Using the pastry brush or your finger, dab a tiny bit of water carefully around each spoonful of filling.

Fold over the square, corner to corner, to create a filled triangle, and press the edges together to seal. Watch out for any air pockets that may have formed, pushing any bubbles of air away and out of the pasta, making sure you pinch the edges together firmly.

Trim the edges of each triangle with a knife for a clean shape, or use a *ravioli* cutter to create a zig-zag edge.

Lift each *triangoli* onto the dusted tray, then dust again with a little more coarse semolina while you roll and fill the next batch of dough.

TRIANGOLI WITH BROAD BEANS, RICOTTA & MINT

This is one of my favourite recipes (though I do tend to say that about all of them at one time or another). It's so fresh, and especially nice in early summer when broad (fava) beans are in season. There are no shortcuts here: you must peel the beans after you've blanched them whether you're using fresh or frozen. You can also use fresh or frozen peas – both work really well with ricotta and mint – and peas have the obvious bonus that you don't have to peel them!

400g/14oz spinach egg dough
(page 32)

100g/3½oz broad (fava) beans
(approx. 250g/9oz unpodded
weight)
250g/9oz ricotta
30g/1oz Parmesan, finely grated,
plus extra to serve
zest of 1 lemon
80g/3oz butter
15 mint leaves, shredded, to serve

SERVES 4

Blanch the broad (fava) beans by dropping them into a pan of boiling water for 1 minute, then drain and quickly plunge them into cold water. They'll soon be cool enough to handle so you can peel them.

Place the ricotta and the peeled broad beans in a food processor and blend for 10 seconds until a rough paste is formed. Tip into a bowl. If you are mixing by hand, roughly mash the broad beans, add the ricotta and combine.

Next, add the Parmesan and lemon zest and mix together, then season with freshly ground black pepper and fine sea salt – don't be afraid to season it really well. Cover the bowl with clingfilm (plastic wrap) and leave the filling in the fridge for 30 minutes (it will firm up a little in the cold).

Roll and fill the *triangoli* following the instructions on page 126.

Bring a large pan of water to the boil before adding salt, then drop the *triangoli* into the water, a few at a time, and cook for 1½–2 minutes.

For the butter sauce, pour a ladleful of the pasta cooking water into a wide saucepan and add the butter. It will quickly melt, so keep stirring to create an emulsion.

Lift the *triangoli* out of the water using a slotted spoon and add them to the butter sauce. Toss gently to create a beautiful silky coating over the pasta.

Just before serving, scatter over the shredded mint leaves and finish with a grating of Parmesan over each plate.

CAPPELLETTI

Cappelletti, or 'little hats', are often made from circles, but I like to shape them from squares. The principle is exactly the same, but this way there's less dough wastage and the finished shape looks more like a heart than a little cap. When I make striped *cappelletti* with squid ink and rich egg dough, people often say they look like the yellow and black Batman logo, too.

Follow the steps for making *triangoli* (page 126).

Holding a triangle with the long, folded edge facing away from you, press a finger into the fold to make a small indent.

Push each end of the top two corners together to meet over the indent, then press them firmly together to seal. The pasta should now look like a heart, a Batman logo, a jaunty sailor's hat… or hopefully something similar. The more you make, the easier it becomes.

Lift each *cappelletti* onto the dusted tray, then dust again with a little more coarse semolina while you roll and fill the next batch of dough.

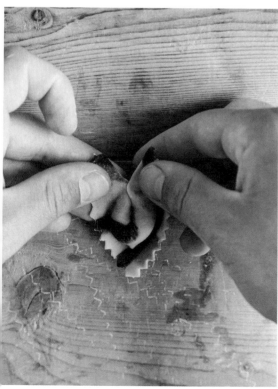

CAPPELLETTI WITH PRAWNS & LEMONY SAMPHIRE SAUCE

I first made these *cappelletti* at work with my friend and fellow chef Holly, as we like to play with flavours from different food cultures. Marinating the prawns in soy sauce brings an Asian flavour to these little pasta hats, which reminds me of eating dumplings. You'll find samphire at the fishmonger's or the supermarket fish counter, but it is seasonal so if you can't get it, use fresh herbs instead – pick the leaves from a good handful of lemon thyme, for example. If you don't want to make two doughs, you could just use the classic egg dough, but the stripes do bring a bit of fun to the presentation.

200g/7oz classic egg dough
    (page 26)
200g/7oz squid ink egg dough
    (page 36)

400g/14oz frozen raw and peeled
    king prawns, defrosted
2 small fresh red chillies, deseeded
    and finely chopped
½ teaspoon fine sea salt
30ml/2 tablespoons soy sauce
100g/3½oz salted butter
100g/3½oz samphire, washed and
    picked from the woody stem
juice of ½ lemon

SERVES 4

Finely chop the prawns and combine with the chillies, sea salt and soy sauce in a large bowl. If you have a food processor, there's no need to chop – just combine everything together into a rough paste and then transfer to a bowl. Leave the mixture to marinate while you make your pasta dough.

Make your stripy dough (page 44), then roll, fill and shape your *cappelletti* (page 130) and set on a semolina-dusted tray.

Bring a large pan of water to the boil before adding salt, and cook the *cappelletti*, a few at a time, for 1½–2 minutes.

For the butter sauce, pour a ladleful of water into a wide saucepan and add the butter. It will quickly melt, so keep stirring to create an emulsion.

Transfer the *cappelletti* into the sauce using a slotted spoon. Gently combine with the sauce, making sure all the *cappelletti* are well coated. Add the samphire and lemon juice and mix everything together, either by gently shaking the pan or turning with a spatula, to avoid breaking any of the *cappelletti*. Loosen the sauce with another half-ladleful of pasta water if necessary. Check the seasoning and serve straight away.

GORGONZOLA & PEAR CAPPELLETTI WITH BROWN BUTTER & WATERCRESS

Pear and Gorgonzola is a classic pairing: a quartered ripe pear with a large slice of this sharp-tasting cheese is a beautiful way to finish a meal. Here, they are combined to create a delicious filling inside these little pasta hats, all coated in nutty brown butter with peppery fresh watercress. I prefer to use Conference pears, but you can use any type as long as they're not overripe – the pears shouldn't be too soft. You can make the filling a little way ahead as it needs time to rest in the fridge; I leave it for a minimum of 30 minutes as it's easier to work with, but beware, if you leave it more than a couple of hours, the pear will turn brown.

200g/7oz spinach egg dough
   (page 32)
200g/7oz classic or rich egg dough
   (pages 26 & 27)

250g/9oz Gorgonzola
70g/2½oz Parmesan, grated
1 small pear, peeled and finely
   chopped into 0.5cm/¼in cubes,
   or coarsely grated
80g/3oz butter
30g/1oz walnuts, chopped, to serve
bunch of watercress, stalks discarded,
   to serve

SERVES 4

In a medium bowl, fork together the Gorgonzola, Parmesan and pear to make a firm and thick mix. Cover the bowl with clingfilm (plastic wrap) and put in the fridge to set for no more than 2 hours.

Meanwhile, make your stripy dough (page 44), then roll, fill and shape your *cappelletti* (page 130) and set on a semolina-dusted tray.

Now make the brown butter. Place a small saucepan on a medium heat and add the butter. Swirl the pan from time to time to make sure the butter is cooking evenly. Cook until the butter browns and you smell its lovely, nutty flavour, then take off the heat and strain into a large saucepan (this is to avoid any dark brown bits spoiling the texture of the sauce).

Bring a large pan of water to the boil before adding salt, and cook the *cappelletti*, a few at a time, for around 2 minutes. You can check they are ready by scooping one out and pinching the corner – if it's nice and soft, then it's done.

Put the pan of brown butter back on the heat, add half a ladleful of the pasta cooking water and give it a quick swirl to blend. Using a slotted spoon, transfer the *cappelletti* to the sauce and mix gently. Scatter the chopped walnuts on top and garnish with fresh watercress.

SPINACH CAPPELLETTI FILLED WITH POTATO, MUSHROOM & THYME

The Polish have a reputation for eating lots of potatoes. I am no exception to this rule and am especially fond of buttery mashed potato (I often put a large spoonful in the bottom of a bowl of Borscht, as a delicious surprise). Here, creamy mashed potato is mixed with mushroom and thyme to fill these little pasta hats. Try to use a mixture of different mushrooms, including dark chestnut, which will give you the best depth of flavour.

400g/14oz spinach egg dough
  (page 32)

450g/1lb potatoes (for mashing)
30ml/2 tablespoons olive oil
1 onion, finely chopped
3 garlic cloves, finely chopped
250g/9oz mixed mushrooms, finely
  chopped
4 sprigs of thyme, leaves picked
½ teaspoon salt
50g/2oz Parmesan, grated, plus
  extra to serve
50g/2oz butter
50g/2oz mascarpone
bunch of parsley, finely chopped

SERVES 4

Boil the potatoes in a pan of salted water until they are just cooked and ready to mash.

In the meantime, heat the olive oil in a frying pan, add the onions and garlic and fry for a couple of minutes. Now add the mushrooms and cook for 7–8 minutes on a medium heat until they are nicely cooked and soft, then add the thyme and season with the salt. Continue to cook on a low heat for another 5 minutes, then take off the heat.

Mash the potato using a ricer or potato masher, then fold in the mushroom mixture, Parmesan and season with freshly ground black pepper, adding more salt if needed. Leave the mixture in the fridge for 30 minutes for the flavours to combine.

Roll, fill and shape your *cappelletti* following the instructions on page 130.

Put a large saucepan on a low heat and add the butter and mascarpone together with 100ml/7 tablespoons of water. Mix until combined to create a smooth, buttery sauce.

At the same time, bring a large pan of water to the boil before adding salt. Drop the *cappelletti* into the boiling water, a few at a time, and cook for around 2 minutes, then use a slotted spoon to transfer them to the sauce, reserving some of the cooking water.

Sprinkle the parsley all over the pasta and gently combine. The sauce should just coat the pasta – you are looking for a consistency similar to double cream, so loosen the sauce with the reserved pasta water if necessary.

Divide between four plates and serve with a chunk of Parmesan to allow people to help themselves.

TORTELLINI

This filled pasta is the ultimate comfort food. *Tortellini* (sometimes referred to as 'belly buttons', *ombellico*) are traditionally filled with meat and served in *brodo* ('broth'). They're fiddly but worth it for the smiles at the table when you serve them. You can freeze them on the tray, as with *ravioli* (page 122).

Prepare a tray or baking sheet dusted with coarse semolina, ready to lay out your finished pasta.

Start with about a quarter of the dough, keeping the rest of it well wrapped. Keep a glass of chilled water and a pastry brush to hand, as the dough can sometimes dry out as it's worked.

Following the method on page 40, roll out your pasta dough, stopping at setting 8.

Cut out evenly sized squares. I think 5–6cm/ 2–2½in squares work best; anything smaller than 5cm/2in will be tricky to work with.

Pipe or place a teaspoonful of filling in the middle of a square.

Using the pastry brush or your finger, dab a tiny bit of water carefully around each spoonful of filling, then fold over the square, corner to corner, to create a filled triangle and press the edges together to seal, watching out for any air pockets, and pushing any bubbles of air away and out of the pasta.

Holding the triangle with the folded long edge towards you, pinch two corners together to form a pleat. It will now look a bit like an admiral's hat. Curl the pleats together around your thumb or forefinger to make a ring. Press the corners firmly together to seal.

Dust with semolina and place on the tray while you roll and fill the next batch of dough.

TORTELLINI WITH SPINACH, RICOTTA & NUTMEG

This is a classic *tortellini* recipe served with a simple butter sauce and a drizzle of balsamic vinegar. I suggest you make half the *tortellini* with rich egg dough (page 27) and half with spinach egg dough (page 32), as it's a fun way to make the plate look colourful. Serve this with a lemon-dressed fresh salad or some peppery rocket (arugula) on the side.

200g/7oz spinach egg dough
  (page 32)
200g/7oz rich egg dough (page 27)

30ml/2 tablespoons olive oil
2 garlic cloves, finely chopped
100g/3½oz spinach leaves, washed
  and chopped
250g/9oz ricotta
30g/1oz Parmesan, grated, plus extra
  to serve
zest of 1 lemon
½ nutmeg, grated
100g/3½oz butter
balsamic vinegar, to serve

SERVES 4

Gently heat the olive oil in a medium saucepan and fry the garlic for a minute or two until it is nice and fragrant, then add the chopped spinach. Continue cooking for another minute or so until the spinach has wilted, then take the pan off the heat and allow to cool.

In a medium bowl, combine the ricotta, Parmesan, lemon zest and nutmeg and season generously with salt and freshly ground black pepper. Mix well, then fold in the cooled spinach. Check the seasoning again and, if you are happy, transfer the mixture to a piping bag (or to a container if you're not going to pipe the filling) and leave in the fridge for at least 30 minutes to firm up.

Roll, fill and shape your *tortellini* following the instructions on page 136.

Bring a large pan of water to the boil before adding salt, then drop the *tortellini* into the water, a few at a time, and boil for 1½–2 minutes.

For the butter sauce, pour a ladleful of the pasta cooking water into a large saucepan and add the butter. It will quickly melt, so keep stirring to create an emulsion.

Transfer the *tortellini* into the sauce using a slotted spoon. Gently combine with the sauce, making sure all the *tortellini* are well coated.

Divide the pasta between four plates, then drizzle with balsamic vinegar and grate some more Parmesan over the top before serving.

AGNOLOTTI DEL PLIN

This pasta originates from Piedmont in Italy and is shaped like neat little folded pillows. *Plin* means 'to pinch', as you pinch the edges together to seal in the filling, and while the filling varies, it is usually based on roasted meat.

Prepare a tray or baking sheet dusted with coarse semolina, ready to lay out your finished pasta.

Start with about a quarter of the dough, keeping the rest of it well wrapped. Following the method on page 40, roll out your pasta dough, stopping at setting 8. Aim for sheets about 10cm/4in wide to avoid wastage.

Fold a sheet in half lengthways, gently press on the fold so that the centre is marked, then spread it out flat again.

Drop teaspoons of filling above the fold line with a thumb-width space between each spoonful, along the length of the dough.

Using a pastry brush or your finger, dab a little water carefully around each spoonful of filling, then fold the dough over the filling so that the long edges meet, lightly pressing down but not sealing the dough fully.

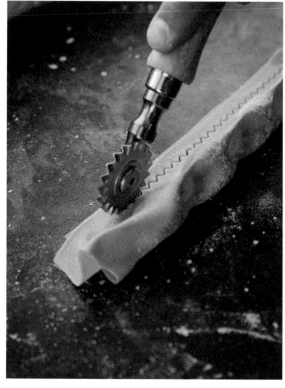

In the spaces between the mounds of filling, pinch the dough together to create a little wall so the shape resembles a wrapped boiled sweet. Pinch all along the row.

Next, using a *ravioli* cutter, cut along the whole length of the dough to seal and trim the long edge.

Now cut between each shape. Roll your cutter from the folded side towards the cut edge; the ridge between the filling will be pushed over to connect with the flat dough beneath to create the characteristic pillow shape of *agnolotti*.

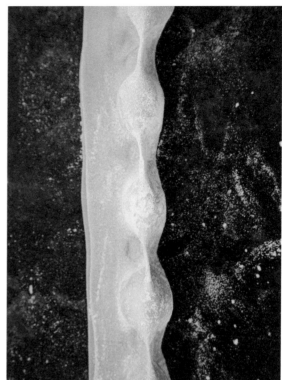

ASPARAGUS & RICOTTA AGNOLOTTI IN BROWN BUTTER

The first asparagus of spring is always so welcome, and I like to eat as much as possible before the short season is over. It's best to buy it from a greengrocer's or local farmers' market if you can, or keep an eye out for a roadside stall if you're lucky enough to live in asparagus country. Mixed with delicate ricotta, the two ingredients really complement one another, while the brown butter brings a nutty flavour to the dish.

400g/14oz classic or rich egg dough
   (pages 26 & 27)

200g/7oz asparagus, ends trimmed
   and stalks peeled
250g/9oz ricotta
50g/2oz Parmesan, grated, plus extra
   to serve
45ml/3 tablespoons olive oil
zest of 2 lemons
1 large or 2 small sprigs of rosemary,
   leaves finely chopped
1 teaspoon salt
60g/2¼oz butter

SERVES 4

Bring a large pan of water to the boil, add salt and blanch the asparagus for 1½–2 minutes, then transfer immediately to a bowl of iced water to help retain its colour. Remove from the water and dry the stems as much as you can.

Cut the tips off the stems and slice them finely lengthways, then set aside.

Roughly chop the remaining asparagus stalks and add to the bowl of a food processor with the ricotta, Parmesan, olive oil, lemon zest and rosemary. Season with the salt and a grinding of black pepper. Blend everything together for 1 minute, then transfer to a small bowl and leave in the fridge for 30 minutes. If you don't have a food processor, simply chop the asparagus finely and combine it with the other ingredients by hand.

Roll, fill and shape your *agnolotti* following the instructions on page 140.

Place a small saucepan on a medium heat and add the butter. Swirl the pan from time to time to make sure the butter is cooking evenly. Cook until the butter browns and you smell its lovely, nutty flavour, then take off the heat and strain into a large saucepan (this is to avoid any dark brown bits spoiling the texture of the sauce).

Bring a large pan of water to the boil before adding salt, and cook the *agnolotti*, a few at a time, for 1½–2 minutes.

Add a small ladleful of the pasta cooking water to the brown butter and put it back on a medium heat. Using a slotted spoon, carefully transfer the pasta to the sauce and gently combine. Loosen the sauce with more pasta cooking water if necessary, then add the sliced asparagus tips for a final few seconds to warm them through. Serve straight away, scattering more Parmesan on top.

CULURGIONES

▼▼▼▼▼▼▼▼▼▼▼▼▼▼▼▼▼▼▼▼▼▼▼▼▼

This is a traditional Sardinian pasta shape, always filled with potato, mint and pecorino. You will need a plain, non-fluted pastry ring cutter about 7–8cm/2¾–3¼in in diameter

Prepare a tray or baking sheet dusted with coarse semolina, ready to lay out your finished pasta.

Start with about a quarter of the dough, keeping the rest of it well wrapped. Following the method on page 40, roll out your pasta dough, stopping at setting 5. Your dough should be pliable but not moist. If it needs to be a little drier, dust with semolina, fold the sheet over and roll again.

Using the ring cutter, cut discs from the sheet of pasta, then lift up and remove the excess cut dough and roll it into a rough ball. Cover this with clingfilm (plastic wrap) so that you can roll it out again later.

Roughly shape a tablespoon of filling in your hands so that it resembles a cocktail sausage. Place in the centre of a circle of dough.

Now pick up a circle of dough in your left hand (or whichever hand you prefer, keeping your other hand for the shaping) and fold the dough over, like a taco, cradling it in your palm between your thumb and forefingers. Working from one end of the dough to the other, push in and pinch the edges together, forming a little pleat. Some of the filling will be pushed out at the open end, but that's fine. Once you've reached the end of the dumpling, simply squeeze to seal the pleats together and form a neat little tip.

Place the dumpling on the dusted tray and continue to shape the rest of the dough. The scraps you rolled into a ball will need to be rolled through the pasta machine again to give you a fresh, smooth sheet to work with.

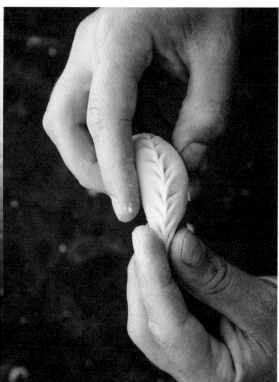

CULURGIONES WITH POTATO, MINT & A SLOW-COOKED TOMATO SAUCE

I discovered *culurgiones* when I went to Sardinia to see my best friend, Luca. He took me to see the February *Sartiglia* – the amazing horseback carnival with costumes and masks for people and horses – an unforgettable day of festivities, jousting, acrobatics, dancing, eating and drinking! We ate this potato-stuffed pasta, another reason the day was so memorable for me as I loved it so much. In Poland, we have dumplings called *pierogi* that are filled with potato, cheese and sometimes pancetta. In Sardinia, this pasta is made with potatoes, cheese and mint. Double carbs – what could be nicer?

400g/14oz vegan semolina dough
    (page 31)

700g/1lb 9oz potatoes, peeled
bunch of mint, stalks and leaves
    separated
80g/3oz pecorino cheese, grated,
    plus extra to serve
½ teaspoon fine sea salt
75ml/5 tablespoons olive oil, plus
    extra for drizzling
5 garlic cloves, thinly sliced
1 x 400g/14oz tin chopped tomatoes,
    or 500g/1lb 2oz cherry tomatoes
handful of torn basil leaves

SERVES 4

Fill a medium-sized pan with cold water and add the potatoes and mint stalks. Season properly with salt, then bring to the boil and cook the potatoes until they are soft and ready to be mashed (about 15 minutes). Drain and discard the mint stalks. Mash the potato using a ricer or potato masher – you want the mash to have a lovely smooth texture. Allow to cool for a few minutes.

Chop the mint leaves finely and combine with the pecorino and mashed potato in a bowl (if the potato is too warm it will discolour the mint, so don't rush). Season with the salt and set aside for at least one hour to allow the potato to really absorb the flavour of the mint, then taste it to check the seasoning.

Next, start on the tomato sauce. In a medium saucepan, heat 45ml/3 tablespoons of the olive oil. Add the garlic and fry on a low heat until fragrant – about 1–2 minutes – then add the tomatoes and stir together. If using fresh tomatoes, once they have softened and split, mash them with the back of a spoon. Continue cooking for 20 minutes on a very low heat so the surface just bubbles from time to time. Season with fine sea salt, add the remaining olive oil and leave on a gentle heat for a further 10–15 minutes.

CONTINUED…

Now the fun starts! While the sauce is cooking, roll, fill and shape the pasta following the instructions on page 144.

Bring a large pan of water to the boil before adding salt. Drop all the *culurgiones* into the boiling water together; they hold their shape well so there's no need to cook in batches. The *culurgiones* are cooked when they bob to the surface, which should take 3 or 4 minutes.

Share the tomato sauce between four warmed pasta bowls. Using a slotted spoon, lift the *culurgiones* from the water and divide them between the bowls. Scatter with the torn basil leaves and grate some pecorino on top.

VEGAN OPTION

Use nutritional yeast instead of the pecorino and adjust the seasoning – it will definitely need more salt to lift the flavour.

MALTAGLIATI

Maltagliati means 'poorly cut' – the scraps of pasta dough left over after shaping – which are traditionally saved to be cooked in a bean soup or *minestrone*. It's a great way of using up bits and pieces of egg pasta dough so there's no waste (unlike pastry, you can't really roll out the scraps again). I generally prefer *maltagliati* to be smaller pieces, but keep whatever you have, large or small, regardless of their shape. You can always cut up any larger pieces, so your shapes are more or less the same size.

Simply gather up all the leftovers and freeze them flat on a tray, then transfer them all to a container and store in the freezer. Alternatively, you can dry them on the table – just leave them uncovered for a couple of hours – before transferring to a freezer container.

When you are almost ready to serve the soup, throw in the *maltagliati* and cook for 2 minutes. The flour from the *maltagliati* will add starch to the soup, thickening it slightly, which I like, but you can thin the soup with a bit more stock (broth), if preferred.

WINTER MINESTRONE

This *minestrone* is a hearty, warming meal in itself, perfect for colder days. The starch from the *maltagliati* and the potatoes thickens it nicely, and if you have a leftover Parmesan rind, it's always good to drop it into the soup to add even more flavour (I keep the rinds in the freezer, as they're a brilliant way of adding depth to soups and risottos).

100g/3½oz *maltagliati* (page 149)

150g/5½oz dried cannellini or borlotti beans, soaked overnight
75ml/5 tablespoons olive oil
1 large onion, sliced or chopped
2 bay leaves
3 garlic cloves, chopped
3 celery sticks, finely diced
½ teaspoon salt
1 leek, chopped into small pieces
1 carrot, finely chopped
2 sprigs of rosemary, leaves picked and chopped
2 sprigs of sage, leaves picked and chopped
1 tablespoon tomato paste
250g/9oz potatoes, cut into 1cm/½in pieces
1 x 400g/14oz tin chopped tomatoes
700ml/1½ US pints vegetable or chicken stock (broth)
Parmesan rind, if you have one
200g/7oz cavolo nero, chard or spinach leaves (tough stalks removed), washed and roughly chopped
Parmesan, *pangrattato* (page 153) or nutritional yeast, to serve

SERVES 4

Drain the soaked beans and add to a medium pan. Cover generously with fresh water, bring to the boil, then cover and simmer for 45–60 minutes. There's no need to season the beans as it will just toughen the skins. When they are soft but still retain some bite, take off the heat and leave to one side.

Meanwhile, in a large heavy-based pan, heat the olive oil and add the onion, bay leaves, garlic, celery and the salt. Fry for 10 minutes on a medium heat, stirring occasionally, until the onion and celery have softened slightly. Add the leek, carrot, rosemary and sage, and continue cooking for a further 5 minutes – the vegetables should smell fantastic by now.

Add the tomato paste and potatoes and fry for another 5 minutes or so, stirring every minute or two. If the veg start to catch a little on the bottom of the pan, don't worry too much as it will give your *minestrone* a nice depth of flavour.

Add the tinned tomatoes, the beans with 400ml/1½ cups of their cooking water, and the vegetable stock (broth). If you have a Parmesan rind, add this too. Turn the heat down so that the soup is simmering gently – you should barely see a bubble popping on the surface – then partially cover with a lid and continue to cook for 1 hour. Take off the heat, fish out the bay leaves and the Parmesan rind (or simply remove them when you serve the soup), then season with fine sea salt and freshly ground black pepper.

Now fold in the leafy greens and the *maltagliati*, cover the pan with the lid and leave everything to sit for 10 minutes – the residual heat from cooking will be enough to soften the pasta and greens.

If the soup is too thick, add a little more stock (broth) or hot water if you like (though this should definitely feel somewhere between a stew and a soup). Serve in shallow bowls with grated Parmesan, *pangrattato* or nutritional yeast sprinkled over the top.

SPRING–SUMMER MINESTRONE WITH MALTAGLIATI

Minestrone – simply, 'big soup' – is a great dish to make with any seasonal vegetables, and in this spring or summer version you can add either late asparagus, early courgettes (zucchini) or the first potatoes and carrots to your base of onions, celery and garlic. You can also add any extra vegetables you have (that half leek you don't know what to do with, or a handful of fresh spinach) – whatever you have to hand really, it's a very easy-going soup. Like most soups, it tastes even better the next day, so it's worth making a large panful. If you do have leftovers, keep a little of the fresh herb salsa to top up each bowl – it really adds a fresh zing.

a large handful or two of *maltagliati* (page 149)
150g/5½oz dried cannellini or borlotti beans, soaked overnight
75ml/5 tablespoons olive oil, plus a little extra for the herb salsa
2 onions, thinly sliced
4 celery sticks, finely diced
2 medium carrots, or a handful of baby carrots, finely diced
3 garlic cloves, finely chopped
2 bay leaves
2 courgettes (zucchini), sliced or cut into cubes
2 medium potatoes, peeled and chopped into small chunks
700ml/1½ US pints vegetable or chicken stock (broth)
bunch of basil, leaves picked
½ bunch of mint, leaves picked
handful of parsley
6 asparagus spears, trimmed and sliced
Parmesan, *pangrattato* (page 153) or nutritional yeast, to serve

SERVES 6

Drain the soaked beans and add to a medium pan. Cover generously with fresh water, bring to the boil, then cover and simmer for 45–60 minutes. There's no need to season the beans as it will just toughen the skins. When they are soft but still retain some bite, take off the heat and leave to one side.

Heat the olive oil in a large, heavy-based pan and fry the onions for 5 minutes until they soften a little, then add the celery, carrots, garlic and bay leaves and continue cooking on a medium heat for 10–15 minutes, turning occasionally to make sure the vegetables don't stick to the bottom of the pan.

Add the courgettes (zucchini) and potatoes and continue to cook for a further 5 minutes, then tip in the beans with 400ml/1½ cups of their cooking water. Pour in the stock (broth) and bring to the boil, then turn the heat down so that the soup is simmering gently – you should barely see a bubble popping on the surface. Partially cover with a lid and continue to cook for 1 hour.

In the meantime, chop all the herbs finely and mix together in a bowl, then add just enough olive oil to create a rough paste. Set aside.

CONTINUED...

At the end of the hour the *minestrone* will have made your kitchen smell beautiful. Remove the bay leaves (if you can find them in the depths of the pan – if not, just watch out for them when serving) and season to taste with fine sea salt and freshly ground black pepper. Finally, turn up the heat, drop the *maltagliati* into the pan with the asparagus and cook for a further 3 minutes.

Turn off the heat and allow the soup to sit for a while – it's not traditional to serve it piping hot. If the soup thickens too much, add a bit more stock (broth) or hot water if you like. Ladle into shallow bowls, add a spoonful of the herby salsa and finish with your favourite topping: Parmesan, *pangrattato* or nutritional yeast.

PANGRATTATO

Quite simply, the Italian for 'breadcrumbs': *pane* is 'bread' and *grattugiato* is 'to grate'. This is a clever way to use up stale bread or the ends of a loaf, and also makes a great vegan alternative to Parmesan or pecorino to finish a dish, while I like to add it for its lovely crunchy texture.

Just put torn pieces of bread into the oven at 160°C fan/350°F/gas mark 4 (ideally when you are already roasting something else) for about 20 minutes – you want the bread to brown a little, but the important thing is to make sure that it has dried out properly. I don't add olive oil at this stage as the bread won't crisp up fully.

Remove from the oven, let the bread cool completely, then add it to the bowl of a food processor. If you process it when it's still slightly warm, it will just become soggy, which isn't what you want at all.

What you add to the mix is up to you and will depend on how much bread you've used. For a small amount (4 or 5 slices), I generally add 1 small garlic clove, ½ teaspoon of chilli flakes, a little olive oil, some sea salt flakes and chopped parsley and blitz everything together to make crumbs.

Keep the *pangrattato* in an airtight container (not in the fridge) for a week or so, and add to soups, salads, macaroni or cauliflower cheese, as well as using it to top your pasta.

INDEX

ACKNOWLEDGEMENTS

When I first came to London in 2013 I had no idea I would end up becoming a chef, let alone that I may one day have the opportunity to publish a cookbook. I am so grateful to all the people who have helped me on my way and have made my life feel like a real adventure story.

My warmest thanks to:

Tim Kershaw at Mischkins for giving me a start in the kitchen there, and to Tom Oldroyd, who set me on the path to joining Padella, where Tom Wakefield and Ray O'Connor sparked my passion for making pasta.

All the team at the Store X – Alessio, Tom, Tommy, Alex – you make each day fun, no matter how much work there is to do or how many hungry people to feed. Yorkshire Tea powers our kitchen.

Richard Snapes at the Snapery Bakery, Ravneet Gill at Countertalk and Konrad Jaworski at Pasta Loco for always being supportive and inspirational.

St Ewe eggs, Molino Pasini, Nicolas Alziari and Marcato Pasta for supplying us with the most beautiful produce and pasta machines. Cooking with good ingredients and using quality tools in the kitchen is always a pleasure.

My brilliant publishers, Sarah Lavelle and Harriet Webster, and to everyone at Quadrille. You are a dream team and I have loved working with you to create a book I am so proud of.

Gemma Hayden for designing a book that captures all the joy of making pasta. I hope it will inspire readers everywhere.

India Hobson and Magnus Edmondson. We shared long, hot days in the photography studio with Holly, Katie and Agathe; I didn't know it was possible to work so hard and to laugh so much.

Elizabeth, my happiness and my critic-at-large. We have eaten a lot of pasta together and shared even more with family and good friends – Fiona and Colin, Chris, Sara, Jane, Ami and Keith – you know who you are.

Max, Hanna, Steve and the Walditch crew, who are always ready to share favourite recipes, veg from the kitchen garden and news and views around the dinner table.

Instagram friends all around the world (something that amazes me always), for all the daily pasta conversations and most especially for posting photographs of the pasta you have made at home. We are so lucky when we can eat and share good food with our family and friends around the table, something I am thankful for every day.

MATEO ZIELONKA

Mateo Zielonka, aka The Pasta Man (dubbed so by his Instafans), is chef at 180 The Strand, a collaborative studio and arts space with Soho House. He also heads up The Store X kitchen with his own pasta space. Polish-born, he has worked in London for six years including time at Padella and Polpo. He also teaches pasta classes. You can find some of his pasta videos on Food52, The Feedfeed and Designmilk. This is his first book.

PUBLISHING DIRECTOR Sarah Lavelle

JUNIOR COMMISSIONING EDITOR Harriet Webster

ART DIRECTION AND DESIGN Gemma Hayden

PHOTOGRAPHER India Hobson

SHOOT ASSISTANT Magnus Edmondson

FOOD STYLISTS Mateo Zielonka, Katie Marshall

FOOD STYLIST ASSISTANT Holly-Dawn Middleton-Joseph

PROP STYLIST Agathe Gits

HEAD OF PRODUCTION Stephen Lang

PRODUCTION CONTROLLER Nikolaus Ginelli

First published in 2021 by Quadrille, an imprint of Hardie Grant Publishing

Quadrille
52–54 Southwark Street
London SE1 1UN
quadrille.com

Cataloguing in Publication Data: a catalogue record for this book is available from the British Library.

ISBN: 978 1 78713 619 9

Printed in China